Flow 2.0

Positive Psychology and Well-Being Series

Editor: Stewart I. Donaldson
Managing Editor: Victoria Cabrera

Flow 2.0: Optimal Experience in a Complex World. Honoring Mihaly Csikszentmihalyi's Legacy
Stewart I. Donaldson and Matthew Dubin

Forthcoming

PERMA+4: Building Blocks for Feeling and Doing Well
Stewart I. Donaldson and Victoria Cabrera

Positive Organizational Psychology Interventions: Design & Evaluation, 2nd Edition
Stewart I. Donaldson and Christopher Chen

Flow 2.0

Optimal Experience in a Complex World.
Honoring Mihaly Csikszentmihalyi's Legacy

Stewart I. Donaldson and Matthew Dubin

This edition first published 2025
© 2025 John Wiley & Sons Ltd

All rights reserved, including rights for text and data mining and training of artificial technologies or similar technologies. No part of this publication may be reproduced, stored in a retrieval system, or transmitted, in any form or by any means, electronic, mechanical, photocopying, recording or otherwise, except as permitted by law. Advice on how to obtain permission to reuse material from this title is available at http://www.wiley.com/go/permissions.

The right of Stewart I. Donaldson and Matthew Dubin to be identified as the authors of this work has been asserted in accordance with law.

Registered Office(s)
John Wiley & Sons, Inc., 111 River Street, Hoboken, NJ 07030, USA
John Wiley & Sons Ltd, The Atrium, Southern Gate, Chichester, West Sussex, PO19 8SQ, UK

For details of our global editorial offices, customer services, and more information about Wiley products visit us at www.wiley.com.

Wiley also publishes its books in a variety of electronic formats and by print-on-demand. Some content that appears in standard print versions of this book may not be available in other formats.

Trademarks: Wiley and the Wiley logo are trademarks or registered trademarks of John Wiley & Sons, Inc. and/or its affiliates in the United States and other countries and may not be used without written permission. All other trademarks are the property of their respective owners. John Wiley & Sons, Inc. is not associated with any product or vendor mentioned in this book.

Limit of Liability/Disclaimer of Warranty
While the publisher and authors have used their best efforts in preparing this work, they make no representations or warranties with respect to the accuracy or completeness of the contents of this work and specifically disclaim all warranties, including without limitation any implied warranties of merchantability or fitness for a particular purpose. No warranty may be created or extended by sales representatives, written sales materials or promotional statements for this work. This work is sold with the understanding that the publisher is not engaged in rendering professional services. The advice and strategies contained herein may not be suitable for your situation. You should consult with a specialist where appropriate. The fact that an organization, website, or product is referred to in this work as a citation and/or potential source of further information does not mean that the publisher and authors endorse the information or services the organization, website, or product may provide or recommendations it may make. Further, readers should be aware that websites listed in this work may have changed or disappeared between when this work was written and when it is read. Neither the publisher nor authors shall be liable for any loss of profit or any other commercial damages, including but not limited to special, incidental, consequential, or other damages.

Library of Congress Cataloging-in-Publication Data
Names: Donaldson, Stewart I. (Stewart Ian), author. | Dubin, Matthew, author.
Title: Flow 2.0 : optimal experience in a complex world : honoring Mihaly Csikszentmihalyi's legacy / Stewart I. Donaldson and Matthew Dubin.
Description: Hoboken, NJ : Wiley, 2025. | Series: Positive psychology and well-being | Includes bibliographical references and index.
Identifiers: LCCN 2024041147 (print) | LCCN 2024041148 (ebook) | ISBN 9781394262991 (paperback) | ISBN 9781394263011 (adobe pdf) | ISBN 9781394263004 (epub)
Subjects: LCSH: Csikszentmihalyi, Mihaly. | Positive psychology.
Classification: LCC BF204.6 .D65 2025 (print) | LCC BF204.6 (ebook) | DDC 150.19/88–dc23/eng/20240927
LC record available at https://lccn.loc.gov/2024041147
LC ebook record available at https://lccn.loc.gov/2024041148

Cover Design: Wiley
Cover Images: © UncleFredDesign/Shutterstock, © punsayaporn/Shutterstock, © Blue Flourishes/Shutterstock, © Azazello/Getty Images, © lushik/Getty Images, © Malte Mueller/Getty Images

Set in 10.5/13pt STIXTwoText by Straive, Pondicherry, India

Contents

About the Authors

Stewart I. Donaldson, PhD, is Distinguished University Professor and executive director of the Claremont Evaluation Center (CEC) and the Evaluators' Institute (TEI) at Claremont Graduate University. He is deeply committed to improving lives through positive psychology research, evaluation, and education. He is co-founder of the first PhD and research-focused master's programs in positive psychology at Claremont Graduate University. He mentors many graduate students specializing in positive psychology and evaluation science.

Professor Donaldson serves on the Council of Advisors for the International Positive Psychology Association (IPPA), is faculty advisor for the Student Division of IPPA (SIPPA), served on the IPPA Board of Directors (2013–2017), was chair of IPPA's World Congress of Positive Psychology in Los Angeles (2013), and is president of the Western Positive Psychology Association (WPPA).

He has published hundreds of peer reviewed articles, chapters, evaluation reports, and more than 20 books on positive psychology and evaluation science topics, including *Flow 2.0: Optimal Experience in a Complex World. Honoring Mihaly Csikszentmihalyi's Legacy* (2024, this volume); *Well-being and Success for University Students: Applying PERMA+4* (2024); *Positive Organizational Psychology*

Interventions: Design and Evaluation (2021); *Positive Psychological Science* (2020); *Toward a Positive Psychology of Relationships* (2018); *Scientific Advances in Positive Psychology* (2017); and *Applied Positive Psychology* (2011).

Professor Donaldson has been honored with many career achievement awards for his research and evaluation contributions, including the 2021 IPPA Fellow Award, 2019 IPPA Work and Organizations Division Exemplary Research to Practice Award, and the 2019 SIPPA Inspiring Mentor Award.

Matthew Dubin, PhD, is an organizational psychologist and one of the leading practitioners on enabling flow at work. He is the co-founder of The Venn Collective, a culture and leadership development consultancy that utilizes flow-based principles to create peak performing organizations. Dr. Dubin has worked largely with the sports, media, and entertainment industries, partnering with the Los Angeles Lakers, the National Women's Soccer League, FanDuel, the Toronto Blue Jays, FOX Sports, and Paramount, among others.

Dr. Dubin completed his PhD in Psychology under the tutelage of Dr. Csikszentmihalyi at Claremont Graduate University, where he was awarded the inaugural Mihaly Csikszentmihalyi Dissertation Award for Excellence in Positive Psychology for his research on cultivating flow in the workplace. He received his BA from the University of Michigan, where he was introduced to the theory of flow by his first career mentor, Dr. Christopher Peterson.

He is based in Los Angeles, where he lives with his wife and two young children. Outside of work, Dr. Dubin finds flow from playing basketball and guitar, baking desserts with his daughter, having meaningless sports arguments with friends, and, of course, talking and reading about flow.

Preface

The world continues to evolve at an accelerating pace. In recent years, technologically enhanced remote and hybrid learning environments and workplaces, as well as regular interactions with artificial intelligence and social robots, have become commonplace. Many would agree that we are living at a different time with new daily challenges than when Professor Mihaly Csikszentmihalyi introduced us to *Flow: The Psychology of Optimal Experience* (1990) and his vision for the science of positive psychology.

> *People who learn to control inner experience will be able to determine the quality of their lives, which is as close as any of us can come to being happy.*
>
> *(Csikszentmihalyi 1990 in* Flow: The Psychology of Optimal Experience)

> *Positive psychology is "a science of positive subjective experience, positive individual traits, and positive institutions that promises to improve quality of life and prevent the pathologies that arise when life is barren and meaningless."*
>
> *(Seligman & Csikszentmihalyi 2000, p. 5).*

Professor Csikszentmihalyi taught us so much more about life than we can share in this book, which is intended to honor his legacy and show how some of his major contributions can be extended to improve our lives in 2024 and beyond.

I (Stewart Donaldson) was first inspired by Professor Csikszentmihalyi's work when I read *Beyond Boredom and Anxiety: Experiencing Flow in Work and Play* (Csikszentmihalyi 1975) when I was a graduate student in the late 1980s. I was instantly a fan of his work and have followed it closely ever since. I was thrilled when I heard he was leaving the University of Chicago to join us on the faculty at Claremont Graduate University (1999). But, I never imagined we would become very close friends and colleagues and I would be afforded the honor and amazing opportunity to work closely with Mihaly for approximately 20 years on so many fruitful projects. For example, along with our colleague Jeanne Nakamura, we designed and implemented the first research-oriented PhD and MA programs in 2006 at Claremont Graduate University, which became more popular and successful than we could have ever imagined. Together, we led the World Congress of Positive Psychology in Los Angeles in 2013, created the Western Positive Psychology Association the same year, served on boards together, traveled around the world to many different positive psychology conferences, served on many positive psychology dissertation committees, and published two editions of our book *Positive Psychology Science: Improving Everyday Life, Well-being, Work, Education, and Societies Across the Globe* (2020) among many other enriching flow-producing activities. This 20-year friendship and collaboration has been the highlight of my academic career.

I (Matthew Dubin) first came across Mihaly's genius as an undergrad at the University of Michigan. I was introduced to the concept of flow in Dr. Christopher Peterson's (one of my other heroes and mentors) Positive Psychology course. It is often hyperbole to say one particular thing "changed my life," but reading *Flow* truly did. It was through his teachings that I finally had the language to understand the best moments of my life, and the types of experiences I was constantly seeking. Having grown up in Southern California and knowing I wanted to return home after four winters in Michigan, and then hearing that Mihaly was a co-founder of the only doctorate in Positive Psychology program in the nation, it felt like fate. When I walked into his office for the first time in 2011, seeing piles of thousands of papers strewn across his desk and him leaning back in his chair with his infectious smile, I felt such a sense of calm. I had so many questions for him, but he would always turn the conversation back to me, my interests, and my ideas. Truly the most humble man I've ever met. He had absolutely zero ego about the concept of flow and only was interested in exploring it as an idea outside of himself, not seeking any credit or attention. It reminded me how certain songs become so significant that they seem to belong to everyone, as though the original artist provided a gift to the world. As my advisor and the chair of my dissertation committee, Mihaly made himself available for countless additional conversations in that same office over the next eight years, many of which I count among the peak flow experiences of my life. He cared so much about his students, and truly supported them all as whole people with complex outer and inner lives. Since his passing, I still feel his presence every day, and, when confronted with a complex decision, think: "What would Mihaly do or say here?" The best part of writing this book, by far, was feeling like he was here with me every time I sat down to write. He was a giant in the field, but also a true giant of humanity.

We were both devastated when we heard the sad news that the father of flow was no longer with us in the physical world. It was so difficult to talk about this personal and professional loss, and to help our public relations team at Claremont Graduate University (CGU) share the story of his amazing positive influence on people around the world.

***

The CGU press release is published here, in part, with permission:

Passings: Mihaly Csikszentmihalyi, the 'Father of Flow,' 1934–2021

THE SEARCH FOR HAPPINESS: Mihaly Csikszentmihalyi at the podium during the 2018 Western Positive Psychology Association conference in Claremont.

BACK IN THE 1950s, when Mihaly Csikszentmihalyi was 16 and traveling in Switzerland (but with no money to enjoy skiing or even go to a movie), he heard about a free lecture in Zurich. The lecture was on the topic of flying saucers.

It sounded entertaining to him, he told a TED audience in 2004. Since it was free, he decided to go.

The man he heard that night didn't talk about aliens from outer space. He spoke about how the psyches of Europeans had been so deeply traumatized by World War II that they projected UFOs into the skies.

It was a coping mechanism, the man said, a way of finding order in the inexplainable chaos of war.

Csikszentmihalyi had no idea that the lecturer that night was Carl Jung—but hearing Jung stayed with him long after he moved to the United States at the age of 22. He'd witnessed that wartime trauma himself—his own family suffered the loss of his two older brothers—and it instilled in him a deep desire to study psychology and understand what a meaningful life can be.

That inquiry into life's meaning and purpose resulted in an acclaimed professional career that, over many years, garnered him much praise and attention as a founder of the popular and growing field of positive psychology and as the "father of flow," which refers to the optimal psychological state when one is fully immersed in an activity.

The CGU community is mourning the loss of this pioneering figure known fondly on campus as "Mike C." According to a message posted on Facebook by the family, Csikszentmihalyi died last week on October 20, surrounded by his family in his Claremont home. Isabella, his wife of 60 years, was at his bedside. He was 87.

Reactions: On-Campus & Beyond

CGU President Len Jessup and School of Social Science, Policy & Evaluation (SSSPE) Dean Michelle Bligh delivered the sad news of Mike's passing in messages to the entire university community as well as to the members of the Division of Organizational & Behavioral Sciences (DBOS).

For CGU's Stewart Donaldson, who worked with Csikszentmihalyi to create the university's trailblazing program in positive psychology, the news was still a shock even though he knew Mike had been ailing in recent years.

He said it felt like losing a parent.

"I haven't felt this low since my dad died," said Donaldson, who is a University Distinguished Professor and directs the Claremont Evaluation

Center. "He was such a trustworthy friend, and I learned so much from him. He was one of the most present people I knew. He'd just listen to you, and he was in the moment, in the flow, and I think that's because he'd studied it for so long and knew how to live life in that optimal state."

Word also spread to many beyond campus, including Martin Seligman, Emeritus Zellerbach Family Professor of Psychology at the University of Pennsylvania. Seligman co-founded the field of positive psychology with Mike in the late 1990s.

Seligman, who received the news as his first grandson was being born, said it plunged him into "the profoundest grief at losing my colleague and friend Mike" even as he was experiencing the elation of becoming a grandparent.

Similar sentiments were expressed on social media by former colleagues and students and in the Hungarian press. *Boing Boing* referred to him as "legendary"; *The Budapest Times* and *Hungary Today* hailed him as the "Flow Theory Architect." *Hungary Daily News* celebrated his career and called him a psychologist "whose theory conquered the world."

Early Years, Move to Claremont

Born in 1934 in Fiume, Italy (now Rijeka, Croatia), Csikszentmihalyi was the son of Hungarian diplomat Alfred Csikszentmihalyi (né Hausenblasz) and Edith Jankovich de Jeszenicze. As a refugee in post-war Rome, he attended the Classical Gymnasium Torquato Tasso and developed a deep interest in psychology.

In 1956, he moved to the United States to study psychology at the University of Chicago and wrote his doctoral dissertation on artistic creativity with creativity scholar Jacob W. Getzels. During that time, he met Isabella Selega, a graduate student in Russian history. They married in 1961, and Csikszentmihalyi taught at Illinois' Lake Forest College before joining the Chicago faculty in 1971.

In the 1990s, with his retirement from Chicago, the Drucker School's Jean Lipman Blumen recruited him to come to Claremont and teach psychology and management. With his arrival and with the droves of psychology students that headed down to his Drucker office, it was clear that something special was happening on campus. So when he was given an offer from USC to start his own program, Donaldson said he asked Mike to stay and do it at CGU instead under the auspices of DBOS. Mike agreed.

Together, Donaldson recalled, they thought that their positive psychology program would simply be a small concentration that would fit with the division's other programs, but, he added, "it just took off and, many hundreds of graduates later, it has taken on an incredible life all of its own."

"Flow," Innovations, Publications, & Awards

Csikszentmihalyi is best known for his work on the concept of "Flow," which describes a state of optimal experience in which one's skills match the challenges of a situation, and for his role as a founder of positive psychology.

Underlying much of this work was his innovative and groundbreaking use of pagers and questionnaires to produce a database based on people's self-reports of their ordinary experiences.

Flow: The Psychology of Optimal Experience became a bestseller in 1990, which presented his conclusions based on that database in a warm, humanistic prose style. His other books, *The Evolving Self* (1993), *Creativity* (1996), and *Good Business* (2003), expanded on his theories in a variety of directions.

Because Csikszentmihalyi's approach generated a cross-section of daily experience, his analysis paid more attention to experiences of positive states–like enjoyment or creativity–than many of his predecessors. That work formed the theoretical background of his collaboration with Seligman.

Together, in 2000, they published an influential article in *American Psychologist*, the flagship journal of the American Psychological Association, that introduced the profession to positive psychology. That work was recognized with Csikszentmihalyi's appointment as a Fellow of the American Academy of Arts and Sciences and his selection for the 2009 Clifton Strengths Prize and the 2011 Széchenyi Prize.

Seligman–who served as the APA's president in 1998–recalled how he asked Mike to join him in writing their pioneering journal article.

"Mike had played such an enormous role in helping me prepare my theme for the APA presidency," he recalled, "that I prevailed on him to be the joint author of that article."

Other awards and distinctions include his receipt, in 2014, of the Grand Cross of the Order of Merit of the Republic of Hungary. Csikszentmihalyi also has enjoyed a robust following online; Since the first appearance of his 2004 TED Talk, "Flow, the secret to happiness," it has received some 6,693,254 views.

https://www.cgu.edu/news/2021/10/passings-mihaly-csikszentmihalyi-the-father-of-flow-1934-2021/

***

We (Stewart & Matthew) decided we wanted to honor Mihaly for all he gave to us and the thousands of other people whose lives he touched and improved in so many ways. After considering a number of ways to do that, we landed on the idea of writing this book together.

After all, Mihaly taught us:

> *Writing gives the mind a disciplined means of expression.*
> *(Csikszentmihalyi 1991 in* Flow: The Psychology of Optimal Experience*)*

How can some of Professor Csikszentmihalyi's profound ideas and contributions help us and people today navigate our increasingly complex lives and world? This is the question we try to answer in the chapters of this book. Our aim is to help keep Mihaly's legacy alive and well, and to help share his insights and rich depth of knowledge that he has gifted us so we can have more optimal experiences and fulfilling lives in the days and years ahead.

Stewart I. Donaldson
Claremont, California

Matthew Dubin
Los Angeles, California

1

The New Science and Practice of Positive Psychology

PERMA+4, Optimal Experience, and Beyond

Control of consciousness determines the quality of life.
(Csikszentmihalyi 1990 in Flow: The Psychology of Optimal Experience*)*

Our colleague, mentor, and great friend Mihaly Csikszentmihalyi (1934–2021) had a wonderful life that propelled him to make lasting impacts on us, many other colleagues and students, and societies across the globe. During the last two decades of his life, he created with his colleagues a new science and practice of positive psychology (Donaldson et al. 2023). Positive psychology is "a science of positive subjective experience, positive individual traits, and positive institutions that promises to improve quality of life and prevent the pathologies that arise when life is barren and meaningless" (Seligman and Csikszentmihalyi 2000, p. 5).

While other pioneers in psychology, such as William James and Abraham Maslow, set the stage for contemporary positive psychology, it was not until the turn of this century that the late Mihaly Csikszentmihalyi and his partner Martin Seligman provided a clear vision for how to develop a body of empirical evidence and a rigorous science of positive psychology began to emerge (Donaldson et al. 2023). Mihaly also clearly described the intangible and almost invisible difference that positive psychology is likely to make toward our understanding of what it means to be human and positive psychology's potential to give us new hope for the future of humankind (Csikszentmihalyi 2020). He inspired us with

Flow 2.0: Optimal Experience in a Complex World. Honoring Mihaly Csikszentmihalyi's Legacy, First Edition. Stewart I. Donaldson and Matthew Dubin.
© 2025 John Wiley & Sons Ltd. Published 2025 by John Wiley & Sons Ltd.

his view that "this new perspective in psychology, positive psychology, should guarantee a rewarding life to those who choose to pursue it."

The Evidence Base

Since Mihaly and his colleagues provided us with a vision for evidence-based positive psychology, there have been more than two decades of peer-reviewed science on positive psychology topics, supporting a thriving evidence-based practice to assess, develop, and care for the building blocks of well-being and positive functioning (Donaldson et al. 2023). There is also now sound experimental evidence showing that positive psychology interventions (PPIs), intended to improve the building blocks of well-being and positive functioning in life, are efficacious on average, and work very well under specific conditions (Donaldson et al. 2021).

After an extensive examination of the empirical evidence generated during the first decade of positive psychology, Seligman (2011) developed a framework for the routes or building blocks to consider when one wants to develop and care for well-being. He called this framework PERMA, and argued that well-being can be actively developed through pursuing five measurable building blocks:

1) **Positive emotions**. Experiencing happiness, joy, love, gratitude, etc. in the here and now.
2) **Engagement**. Being highly absorbed or *experiencing flow* while engaged in the activities of one's life.
3) **Relationships**. Having the ability to establish and maintain positive, mutually beneficial relationships with others, characterized by experiences of love and appreciation.
4) **Meaning**. The experience of being connected to something larger than the self or serving a higher purpose.
5) **Accomplishment**. Experiencing a sense of mastery over a particular domain of interest or achieving important or challenging life/work goals.

In 2018, Seligman refined the PERMA framework and argued that these five building blocks are not exhaustive, and acknowledged that additional evidence-based building blocks might improve the framework. Donaldson (2019), Donaldson and Donaldson (2021b), and Donaldson et al. (2020) conducted an extensive systematic literature review, meta-analysis, and a range of qualitative assessments in order to determine if and how the framework could be extended, making it especially relevant for work-related contexts and for individuals living in challenging environments (e.g., poor physical and psychosocial conditions with challenges of inequity and poverty). Their main aim was to determine which additional elements seemed likely to contribute to well-being and positive functioning over and above the original five elements. They found that four additional building blocks could explain additional variance in well-being and positive functioning and could thus be considered for inclusion into the PERMA framework (Donaldson and Donaldson 2021b; Donaldson et al. 2020). These four new building blocks included:

1) **Physical health**. Operationalized as a combination of high levels of biological, functional, and psychological health assets.
2) **Mindset**. Adopting a growth mindset characterized by an optimistic, future-oriented view of life, where challenges or setbacks are seen as opportunities to grow. This may also be a function of positive psychological capital, perseverance, and/or grit.
3) **Environment**. The quality of one's physical environment (which includes spatiotemporal elements, such as access to natural light, fresh air, physical safety, and a positive psychological climate), aligned to the preferences of the individual.
4) **Economic security**. Perceptions of financial security and stability are required to satisfy individual needs.

The expanded framework (Figure 1.1) is referred to as PERMA+4 (see Donaldson et al. 2022 for a detailed account of the development and validation of PERMA+4).

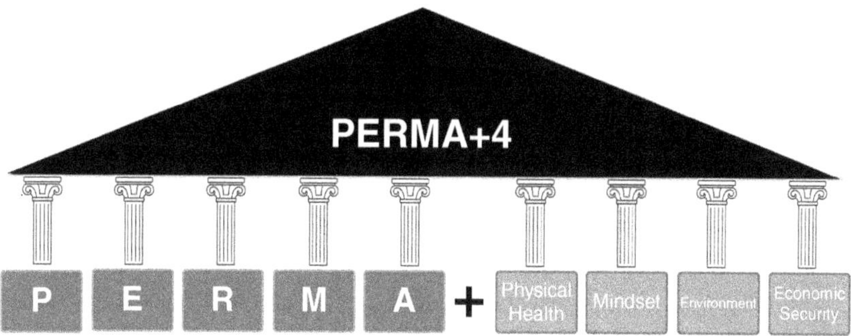

Figure 1.1 PERMA+4.

PERMA and PERMA+4 Frameworks

The evidence continues to mount for the value of the PERMA and PERMA+4 frameworks for guiding future positive psychology research and practice (Cabrera and Donaldson 2023; Donaldson et al. 2022). For example, more than a decade's worth of empirical research underpinning the relationships between the individual elements of PERMA and well-being (e.g., Kern et al. 2014; Kern et al. 2015; Seligman 2018), often measured by the PERMA-Profiler (Butler and Kern 2016), provided the foundational base from which to extend and build the more holistic framework PERMA+4.

The PERMA+4 framework has also been subjected to rigorous empirical investigation. Donaldson (2019) and Donaldson and Donaldson (2021b) developed and evaluated the Positive Functioning at Work (PFW) scale, which aimed to measure the nine building blocks of the PERMA+4 model. The results demonstrated the convergent, discriminant, criterion, predictive, and incremental forms of validity with other related measures (Satisfaction with Life: Diener et al. 1985; PsyCap: Luthans et al. 2007) and performance measures (Positive Work Role Performance: Griffin et al. 2007), as well as measurement invariance across job function (Donaldson and Donaldson 2021b).

PERMA+4, as measured by the PFW Scale, has also been found to predict essential work outcomes, such as turnover intentions, job-related affective well-being, plus individual, team, and organizational adaptivity, proactivity, and organizational proficiency (Donaldson and Donaldson 2021a,b), as well as academic success (Weiss et al. 2024). Furthermore, a series of multi-trait multi-method (MTMM) studies have been conducted to further validate PERMA+4 as an evidence-based framework, and clearly showed that PERMA+4 scores predict well-being and positive functioning beyond self-report and mono-method bias (see Donaldson and Donaldson 2021a; Donaldson et al. 2021).

Although more empirical work is ongoing to test the generalizability of the framework, the research on PERMA and PERMA+4 has been encouraging so far (Cabrera and Donaldson 2023). This evidence-informed framework shows great potential to help determine the needs of students, workers, leaders, and organizations, and to guide the design and evaluation of future positive psychology interventions and applications (Donaldson and Chen 2021).

It is important to keep in mind Mihaly's wise quote when applying PERMA+4 to your life:

> *A joyful life is an individual creation that cannot be copied from a recipe.*
>
> *(Csikszentmihalyi 1990, Preface)*

The PERMA+4 building blocks of well-being and positive functioning provide an evidence-informed framework from which people can pick and choose which dimensions to strengthen and care for at any given time in their lives. Some of these building blocks are likely to be more valuable to some individuals than others at a particular point in time. The next wave of positive psychological science would greatly advance the field if it could sort out the interconnections and interactions between the PERMA+4 building blocks (see Cabrera 2024).

Flow 2.0, Optimal Experience, and Beyond

In the new PERMA+4 framework, which draws on and integrates many of the positive psychology research findings to date, engagement (including flow and optimal experience) has been shown to be a powerful building block of well-being and positive functioning. In the remaining chapters this book, we are going to focus in-depth on what we have learned about the engagement building block of well-being and positive functioning. Specifically, we are going to review what Mihaly has taught us about being fully engaged in our lives and living a good life with a healthy amount of flow and optimal experiences. In addition, we are going to explore ways the world has changed since the concept of flow was first developed and studied, and provide some of the latest research and insights about living in Flow 2.0 in our new high-paced, rapidly changing, and largely hybrid world.

We first review what Mihaly has taught us about the basics of flow and optimal experience. This chapter is intended to be an introduction for those who have not read his classic *Flow: The Psychology of Optimal Experience* (Csikszentmihalyi 1990), or a refresher for those who read this work long ago and would like to apply it more in their lives now and in the future. The third chapter explores how we flow together. Social, team, or collective flow has important implications for both our complex social and work lives in our changing societies. Next, we take a deep dive into how Mihaly influenced the world of work through positive psychology and flow. Many of his contributions teach us about what is good work and positive career development, as well as how we can function at our best and experience high levels of well-being and peak performance at work.

Finding flow in sports and leisure pursuits is another area that Mihaly thought and wrote a lot about. We share a range of examples of peak performance emerging when people find flow and get into what many athletes know as the ultimate optimal experience – the *zone*. Our new digital societies often require us to live in a world of multitasking and fragmented attention. In Chapter 6, we explore the future of flow in our hypercomplex and fast-paced digital societies. Finally, the last chapter shares what Mihaly's insights, those shared with us personally in our conversations and professionally in his writings and teaching, mean to us and our lives. We also explore how his insights are relevant for teaching others how to have meaningful optimal experiences, live a good life filled with well-being and positive functioning, and ultimately how to experience human flourishing at both the individual and societal levels in the years ahead.

The main purpose of this book is to honor Mihaly Csikszentmihalyi's legacy, and to make many of his ideas about flow and positive psychology more accessible and usable now and in the years ahead. The following chapters focus on both what we have learned about flow during the past two decades during the development of positive psychological science and how we can apply those findings and principles to help people lead a good life and flourish in the complex and dynamic environments we are likely to find ourselves in (Flow 2.0). We hope you become fully engaged in Flow 2.0 and enjoy many optimal experiences as you navigate and apply the concepts and advice in the chapters to your own life. And, please keep in mind along the way:

> *People who learn to control inner experience will be able to determine the quality of their lives, which is as close as any of us can come to being happy.*
>
> *(Csikszentmihalyi 1990)*

References

Butler, J. and Kern, M. L. (2016). The PERMA-profiler: A brief multidimensional measure of flourishing. *International Journal of Wellbeing*, 6(3): 1–48. https://doi.org/10.5502/ijw.v6i3.526

Cabrera, V. (2024). PERMA+4 building blocks of well-being: A mixed-methods exploration of mechanisms & conditions that enable the subjective well-being of workers. Doctoral dissertation, Claremont, CA: Claremont Graduate University.

Cabrera, V. and Donaldson, S. I. (2023). PERMA to PERMA+4 building blocks of well-being: A systematic review of the empirical literature, *The Journal of Positive Psychology* 3(19): 510–529. https://doi.org/10.1080/17439760. 2023.2208099

Csikszentmihalyi, M. (1990). *Flow: The Psychology of Optimal Experience.* New York: HarperCollins.

Csikszentmihalyi, M. (2020). Positive psychology and a positive worldview: New hope for the future of humankind. In S. I. Donaldson, M. Csikszentmihalyi, and J. Nakamura (eds.), *Positive Psychological Science: Improving Everyday Life, Well-Being, Work, Education, and Society* (2nd ed.). New York: Routledge Academic.

Diener, E., Emmons, R. A., Larsen, R. J., and Griffin, S. (1985). The satisfaction with life scale. *Journal of Personality Assessment* 49(1): 71–75. https://doi.org/10.1207/s15327752jpa4901_13. PMID: 16367493

Donaldson, S. I. (2019). *Evaluating Employee Positive Functioning and Performance: A Positive Work and Organizations Approach.* Doctoral dissertation. Claremont, CA: Claremont Graduate University.

Donaldson, S. I. and Chen, C. (2021). *Positive Organizational Psychology Interventions: Design and Evaluation.* Hoboken, NJ: John Wiley & Sons.

Donaldson, S. I. and Donaldson, S. I. (2021a). Examining PERMA+4 and work role performance beyond self-report bias: Insights from multitrait-multimethod analyses. *Journal of Positive Psychology* 17(6): 1–10. https://doi.org/10.1080/17439760.2021.1975160

Donaldson, S. I. and Donaldson, S. I. (2021b). The positive functioning at work scale: Psychometric assessment, validation, and measurement invariance. *Journal of Wellbeing Assessment* 4: 181–215. https://doi.org/10.1007/s41543-020-00033-1

Donaldson, S. I., Cabrera, V., and Gaffaney, J. (2021). Following the science to generate well-being: Using the highest quality experimental evidence to design interventions. *Frontiers in Psychology* 12. https://www.frontiersin.org/journals/psychology/articles/10.3389/fpsyg.2021.739352/full.

Donaldson, S. I., Gaffaney, J., and Caberra, V. (2023). The science and practice of positive psychology: From a bold vision to PERMA+4. Invited for C. Markey and H. S. Friedman (eds.), *The 3rd Edition of the Encyclopedia of Mental Health*. Cambridge, MA: Academic Press.

Donaldson, S. I., Heshmati, S., Young, J. Y., and Donaldson, S. I. (2020). Examining building blocks of wellbeing beyond PERMA and self-report bias. *Journal of Positive Psychology* 17(6): 811–818. https://doi.org/10.1080/17439760.2020.1818813

Donaldson, S. I., van Zyl, L. E., and Donaldson, S. I. (2022). PERMA+4: A framework for work-related wellbeing, performance and positive organizational psychology 2.0. *Frontiers in Psychology* 12: 817244. https://doi.org/10.3389/fpsyg.2021.817244

Griffin, M. A., Neal, A., and Parker, S. K. (2007). A new model of work role performance: Positive behavior in uncertain and interdependent contexts. *Academy of Management Journal* 50(2): 327–347. https://doi.org/10.5465/amj.2007.24634438

Kern, M. L., Waters, L., Adler, A., and White, M. (2014). Assessing employee wellbeing in schools using a multifaceted approach: Associations with physical health, life satisfaction, and professional thriving. *Psychology* 5: 500–513. https://doi.org/10.4236/psych.2014.56060

Kern, M. L., Waters, L. E., Adler, A., and White, M. A. (2015). A multidimensional approach to measuring wellbeing in students: Application of the PERMA framework. *Journal of Positive Psychology* 10(3): 262–271. https://doi.org/10.1080/17439760.2014.936962

Luthans, F., Avolio, B., Avey, J., and Norman, S. (2007). Positive psychological capital: Measurement and relationship with performance and satisfaction. *Personnel Psychology* 60: 541–572. https://doi.org/10.1111/j.1744-6570.2007.00083.x

Seligman, M. E. P. (2011). *Flourish*. Simon & Schuster.

Seligman, M.E.P. (2018). PERMA and the building blocks of well-being. *Journal of Positive Psychology* 13(4): 333–335. https://doi.org/10.1080/17439760.2018.1437466

Seligman, M. E. P. and Csikszentmihalyi, M. (2000). Positive psychology: An introduction. *American Psychologist* 55(1): 5–14. https://doi.org/10.1037/0003-066X.55.1.5

Weiss, E. L., Donaldson, S. I., and Reece, A. (2024). Well-being as a predictor of academic success in student veterans and factor validation of the PERMA + 4 well-being measurement scale. *Journal of American College Health*. https://doi.org/10.1080/07448481.2023.2299417

Part I

What Mihaly Taught Us About Flow

2

The Basics of Flow and Optimal Experience

Time confetti. This concept refers to the bits of seconds and minutes we're losing by splitting our attention across multiple screens and tasks at one time. A text here, an email there, and social media everywhere take us out of what we're doing at any given moment, creating attentional fragments that don't amount to a meaningful experience. The term was coined by author and productivity expert Brigid Schulte (2020), who wrote the bestselling book *Overwhelmed: Work, Love and Play When No One Has the Time*. The state of flow, on the other hand, is the opposite of time confetti. Flow is complete immersion and energized focus on a singular endeavor, creating an experience that feels like a melody of notes that create harmony together. Flow creates meaningful experiences, where moments fit together seamlessly and we are able to function at the very peak of our powers. When in flow, nothing else matters besides the experience itself, and it is so inherently enjoyable that we seek these moments again, and again, and again. It doesn't matter what it is – it can be work, leisure, sports, or art. We can be alone, with one other person, or with a group of thousands. Flow is there for the taking if we seek it with intention and patience.

However, our modern world is designed to keep us out of flow. We are in the attention economy, and finding flow is all about focusing our attention. Social media platforms are all battling for as much of our attention as they can get. Their algorithms are designed to get our attention and keep it for as long as possible. There's a reason why when an episode of a Netflix show ends, the next one starts without us having to

Flow 2.0: Optimal Experience in a Complex World. Honoring Mihaly Csikszentmihalyi's Legacy, First Edition. Stewart I. Donaldson and Matthew Dubin.
© 2025 John Wiley & Sons Ltd. Published 2025 by John Wiley & Sons Ltd.

lift a finger. Our flow experiences, which we create on our own, mean less time spent with these distractions.

When Mihaly wrote the seminal book on flow in 1990, few could have predicted the number of attentional barriers to flow that now exist 30 years later. Because of this, his concept has taken on even more profound resonance as we all seek to not only perform our best but feel our best as we continue to grapple with the ramifications of a global pandemic. What makes Mihaly's theory so revolutionary is that it is utterly timeless. No matter what our society is going through, no matter where we live or how old we are, the pursuit of flow will always be a fundamental part of the human experience.

So, whether you're into sports, music, reading, baking, gardening, gaming, chatting with friends, or any other physical or mental endeavor, you've probably been in flow. Understanding how to enter flow, and what it looks like when we do, can help us find flow more proactively and consistently, especially when engaging in things we wouldn't necessarily choose to do, like work.

Mihaly created the conditions and characteristics of the experience that have held up tremendously well since his original flow studies in the 1970s. As Mihaly says with his trademark humility: "To call it a 'discovery' is perhaps misleading, for people have been aware of it since the dawn of time. Yet the word is appropriate, because even though my finding itself was well known, it had not been described or theoretically explained by the relevant branch of scholarship, which in this case happens to be psychology" (Csikszentmihalyi 1990, p. 2). To understand how to best achieve flow in 2024 and into the future, it's important to understand what these original characteristics he "discovered" are and how they can best be applied to our own interests, as well as our professional and personal life circumstances.

Conditions of the Flow Experience

Clear Goals

To enter a state of flow, it's essential that we know what we're trying to accomplish. One of the reasons that sports remain such a prime example of flow is that the goals of competition are crystal clear: Win the game, make the shot, complete the pass, etc. Same with baking, for example: You follow a recipe, and you know when it's complete. Music is similar: A guitarist learning to play a new song, for example, has the goal of learning every note of the song and playing it properly. The nature of goals can vary widely. While the example of the guitarist learning a song is a short-term goal that would likely take days or weeks, goals can often take months or years to accomplish. This does not necessarily inhibit the flow experience. On the contrary, a clear long-term goal can provide an avenue for one to experience flow on an enduring basis. For example, a freshman in college who wishes to become a doctor knows that certain courses are required throughout undergraduate schooling, followed by appropriate standardized testing and medical school applications, which lead to medical school and residency before that first-year student will achieve the dream of becoming a practicing physician. This ultimate goal of becoming a doctor has the potential to make each required task leading to that goal a source of flow.

A 62-year-old woman living in the Italian Alps told Mihaly that her most enjoyable experiences were caring for her cows and tending the orchard: "I find special satisfaction in caring for the plants: I like to see them grow day by day. It is very beautiful" (Csikszentmihalyi 1990, p. 55).

Mihaly also describes the study done by Jim Macbeth on flow in ocean cruising, where one elite cruiser describes their goal achievement as follows: "I...experienced a sense of satisfaction coupled with some astonishment that my observations of the very distant sun from an unsteady platform and the use of some simple tables...enable[d] a small island to be found with certainty after an ocean crossing'" (Csikszentmihalyi 1990, p. 55). Flow in our jobs can be challenging, because oftentimes the goals are not as clear. For example, we may know what the organization's goals are, but we don't know how our role fits into them. Both short- and long-term goals need to be clear to experience flow in our professional lives, ideally goals that serve both our individual needs and the organization's interests.

A trivial goal, however, is not necessarily flow conducive if achieving it does not provide joy. As Mihaly says, "If I set my goal to remain alive while sitting on the living-room sofa, I also could spend days knowing that I was achieving it, just as the rock climber does. But this realization would not make me particularly happy, whereas the climber's knowledge brings exhalation to his dangerous ascent" (Csikszentmihalyi 1990, p. 55). A goal that is too easy to achieve will also not be flow conducive, like finishing a cup of coffee or walking from your front door to your car. The goal must hold some sort of intrinsic meaning, joy, and challenge in order for its pursuit to be flow enabling.

Immediate Feedback

Once the goal is clear, its pursuit must then provide immediate feedback of whether we are moving closer to achieving it (Csikszentmihalyi 1990; Nakamura and Csikszentmihalyi 2002; Nakamura and Dubin 2015). The type of feedback we need for achieving flow, however, differs from the more traditional notion we have of feedback when we think about giving or receiving it at work. In this context, feedback generally comes from an external source: our manager. Feedback in the context of flow comes from the flow activity itself, and it comes almost instantaneously. Let's again use the example of a guitarist. Each note the guitarist strums provides feedback: The guitarist is immediately aware of whether she played the right or wrong note and whether she is closer to her goal of learning the song. When feedback is instant, as in the case of the guitarist, flow is more likely to occur since the person pursuing the goal is more likely to stay engaged in the task without external thoughts flooding the mind.

This also helps to explain why some people find it incredibly challenging to cook without a recipe: How are we supposed to know if the dish needs more paprika? Less pepper? More parsley? While some prefer tasting as their source of feedback, the structure that a recipe provides allows us to know whether we are making the right progress. Mihaly says:

> *A tennis player always knows what she has to do: return the ball into the opponent's court. And each time she hits the ball she knows whether she has done well or not. The chess player's goals are equally obvious: to mate the opponent's king before his own is mated. With each move, he can calculate whether he has come closer to this objective. The climber inching up a vertical wall of rock has a very simple goal in mind: to complete the climb without falling. Every second, hour after hour, he receives information that he is meeting that basic goal.*
>
> *(Csikszentmihalyi 1990, p. 54)*

Some tasks, especially in the professional context, do not provide immediate feedback in the way we would hope. For example, let's say a salesperson is working on a PowerPoint pitch presentation deck for a potential client, but they have never completed a deck on their own before. While working on this deck, this person may feel a lack of clarity over what effective progress looks like and what ineffective progress looks like, causing confusion, frustration, and, ultimately, deflation. This is one of the reasons managers hold such profound weight over their employee's experience: It is up to them to provide enough support and feedback in order for their people to eventually feel they can take on the task on their own and have a clear idea of what the final product should look like. Many creative endeavors do not offer clear goals and immediate feedback on the surface: "A composer of music, for instance, may know that he wishes to write a song, or a flute concerto, but other than that, his goals are usually quite vague. And how does he know whether the notes he is writing down are "right" or "wrong" (Csikszentmihalyi 1990, p. 55). While the ability to be open-ended and creative is what often draws creative people to these types of endeavors, ultimately, the composer must create boundaries within the task to know whether the song is progressing, and ultimately, complete. Some songwriters for example, always start with the melody first, then add the lyrics. The structure of the melody allows them to make progress on the lyrics. For others, it's the opposite – the lyrics come first and the melody is then created to fit the structure of the words. Adam Duritz, the lead singer of the band Counting Crows, said in 2015, "It's always music first, or melody and words together, but never words first." Bob Dylan, alternately, said this in a 1978 interview, "I consider myself a poet first and a musician second." These songwriters take different approaches to find flow when creating a song, but they both are able to create their own meaningful structure based on their intrinsic skills and understand whether progress is being made throughout the process.

The Balance Between Challenge and Skill

When we're in flow, our skills continuously meet the challenge provided by the activity. If our level of skill exceeds the opportunity for action, boredom will be the likely result. For example, in the context of work, if an accomplished, competent graphic designer is sent to make photocopies for an afternoon he will likely be bored. If Michael Jordan in his prime (or now, for that matter) played me 1-on-1 in basketball, the lack of challenge I'd provide him would probably cause him severe boredom (or maybe he would somehow still find a way to challenge himself, because the great ones do). However, if the challenge exceeds our skill level, it will likely be a pretty anxiety-provoking experience. That would be me in the 1-on-1 game against MJ. Another

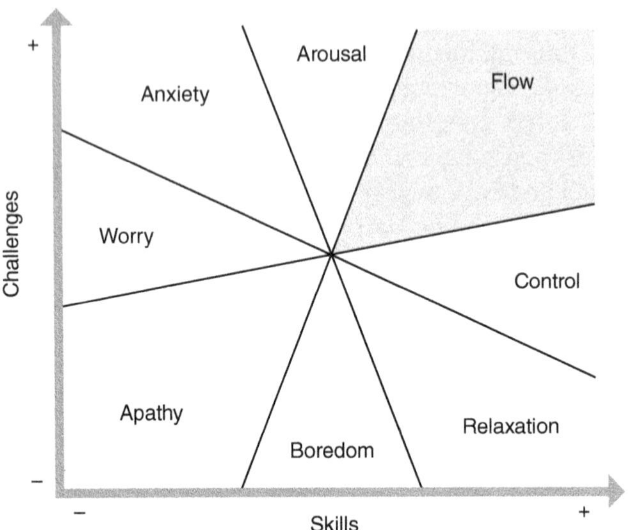

Figure 2.1 Low skill met with high challenge will result in anxiety, and high skill met with low challenge will result in apathy or boredom. *Source:* Nakamura and Csikszentmihalyi (2009) / with permission of Oxford University Press.

example: If an individual who has no experience in public speaking is asked to give a presentation in front of the entire company without rehearsing beforehand, this will likely be an intensely anxiety-provoking experience. Figure 2.1 succinctly describes this balance.

When we engage in a flow task, our skills will inevitably increase, which will lead us to seek increasingly complex challenges to maintain the flow experience in that given activity. For example, if public speaking became a flow activity for the individual in the example above, she may pursue more complex challenges such as speaking in front of larger audiences or speaking on a more diverse set of topics without the aid of PowerPoint slides. Our natural inclination to continuously try and match our skills with challenges is what enables us to achieve our peak potential.

Take the Beatles, for example. Once they mastered the traditional two-minute pop song format of guitars, bass, and drums, their skills had progressed to such a point that it would have become boring to continue doing that. That's when they began to push the envelope of experimentation in the recording studio, using sitar, horns, and tape loops, and continuously seeking new challenges to meet their staggering skill level. This mindset produced some of the great albums of our time, such as

Revolver, *Sgt. Pepper's Lonely Hearts Club Band*, and *Abbey Road*. As Paul McCartney said, "Each time we just want to do something different. After 'Please Please Me,' we decided we must do something different for the next song... Why should we ever want to go back? That would be soft" (Davies 1996, p. 300). The continuous pursuit of greater challenges as we increase our level of skill enables us to fulfill what we are capable of.

While the balance between skill and challenge is essential, our assessment of each is more subjective than we may realize:

> *It is not only the "real" challenges presented by the situation that count, but those that the person is aware of. It is not skills we actually have that determine how we feel, but the ones we think we have...How we feel at any given moment of a flow activity is strongly influenced by the objective conditions; but consciousness is still free to follow its own assessment of the case.*
>
> *(Csikszentmihalyi 1990, pp. 75–76)*

For example, someone with imposter syndrome – "the condition of feeling anxious and not experiencing success internally, despite being high-performing in external, objective ways" (Saymeh 2023) – will often think they lack the requisite skills to meet certain challenges due to their subjective assessment of the situation, not the objective measures of performance. Therefore, if this person felt that they weren't an effective public speaker and they proceeded to give a talk in front of an audience that was extremely well-prepared and delivered, the experience may cause severe anxiety, even if the audience felt the talk was excellent. The experience, therefore, would not be enjoyable, and this person would not naturally seek out these experiences in the future, as a result of his perceived skills not matching his actual, objective skill at the task. On the other end of the spectrum, some individuals are arrogant and overestimate their skills. If another person felt they were an excellent public speaker and therefore loved the experiences of giving a talk to an audience, even if the audience found him to be unengaging and pedantic, the experience may still enable flow for him because of his perceived overestimation of his skills.

Characteristics of the Flow Experience

If the aforementioned conditions are met: Our goals are clear, we're receiving immediate feedback, and our skills are matching the challenge of the situation, we are able enter flow. What does that experience actually feel like? Mihaly, along with his colleagues and peers, continued their flow research and laid out the characteristics of the flow experience to answer this question. The characteristics are as follows:

Complete Concentration

A hallmark of flow is complete concentration in the flow activity, intense absorption, and involvement in the task at hand. In Mihaly's research, he discovered that when individuals experience flow, they forget about potential negative thoughts and distractions and are able to invest all of their psychic attention in the flow task. This sense of intense concentration ideally eliminates the psychic entropy one often feels when unable to devote his attention to external stimuli.

Mihaly defines *psychic entropy* this way:

> *Whenever information disrupts consciousness by threatening its goals we have a condition of inner disorder, or psychic entropy, a disorganization of the self that impairs its effectiveness." While concentrating fully on any external stimuli can temporarily reduce psychic entropy, what differentiates the flow task from other activities is that it builds complexity and ultimately strengthens and completes the self.*
>
> *(Csikszentmihalyi and Csikszentmihalyi 1988)*

In sports, this feeling of complete concentration and absorption in a task is called being "in the zone." Former professional basketball player Ben Gordon describes this feeling on the court:

> *You lose track of time, what quarter it is. You don't hear the crowd. You don't know how many points you have. You don't think. You're just playing. Offensively everything is instinctive. When the feeling starts going away, it's terrible. I talk to myself and say, c'mon, you gotta be more aggressive. That's when you know it's gone. It's not instinctive anymore.*
>
> *(Kennedy 2005, p. 29, as cited in Peterson 2006)*

This "in the zone" feeling has become a colloquial term that many use to describe flow, especially in the sports world. Therefore, think of flow as the psychological theory behind the zone.

Flow activities are so all-consuming that there isn't room for external distraction: "This is one reason why flow improved the quality of experience: the clearly structured demands of the activity impose order and exclude interference of disorder in consciousness" (Csikszentmihalyi 1990, p. 58). When concentration wanes, it is likely that at least one of the preconditions of flow has become ambiguous: The goal is no longer clear, feedback is no longer present or immediate, and our perceived skills no longer match the challenge that the situation presents. Or it may be as simple as our phone buzzing in our pocket that cuts through our concentration. Maintaining concentration means caring for the internal mechanisms of the activity that enable flow (goals, feedback, skill/challenge balance), as well as the external mechanisms that could cause unwanted distraction (putting away technology, turning off notifications, drowning out background noise). These external mechanisms for distraction continue to rise, requiring more discipline to maintain concentration than in the second half of the twentieth century.

Merging of Action and Awareness

When our skills match the challenge of the flow activity and we are in that zone, there is a merging of action and awareness – meaning that all of our attention is given to the activity, and actions feel automatic (Nakamura and Csikszentmihalyi 2002). Even when the task requires considerable mental or physical effort, during flow it feels effortless, as if we are one with the activity.

Jimi Hendrix, one of the greatest guitarists of all time (Figure 2.2), often performed with his eyes closed and said this about playing the guitar: "Don't use your brain to play it, let your feelings guide your fingers (as cited in Uitti 2022). Similarly, rock 'n' roll hall-of-famer Joan Jett described her relationship with her guitar like this: "My guitar is not a thing. It is an extension of myself. It is who I am" (as cited in Earls 2007). That feeling that there is no separation between us and the flow instrument is the merging of action and awareness. Tennis players might feel this way about their rackets; software engineers might feel this way about their laptops.

Loss of Self-Consciousness

Many of today's knowledge workers spend considerable time in virtual meetings. According to research by Microsoft (2023), there has been a 192% increase since 2020 in the amount of time workers spend in meetings. If you're like us, you spend an embarrassing amount of time in the meeting staring at the box of yourself on the screen, making sure you're

Figure 2.2 Jimi Hendrix, one of the all-time great guitarists (1942–1970). *Source:* David Redfern/Getty Images.

coming across in a professional, engaged, and friendly manner. It's a bizarre feeling, basically having a mirror right in front of you when you're supposed to be looking at another person. In those moments, we are completely self-conscious – the feeling of being totally aware of ourselves. However, let's say you're having an incredibly engaging in-real-life conversation with someone, where all of your attention is on the other person and the content of the topic you're discussing. That sense of self-consciousness completely melts away – and we are in flow (Csikszentmihalyi 1985). The ego itself melts away, as one climber describes: "One thing you're after is one-pointedness of mind. You can get your ego mixed up with climbing in all sorts of ways and it isn't necessarily enlightening. But when things become automatic, it's like an egoless thing, in a way" (Csikszentmihalyi 1990, p. 63).

One of the main differences between the current internet/social media era and the era where the seminal flow book came out (1990), is how much more difficult it is to lose our sense of self. We are constantly curating ourselves for our digital world and constantly pushed to turn our existence into a "brand" that is attractive and consumable for friends, potential romantic partners, potential clients, etc. Authentic experiences where we can completely let go and lose that sense of self-consciousness are rare and should be cherished. Even the concept of a selfie, where we can easily take pictures of ourselves with the self-facing view from our phones, is a relatively new phenomenon. If this is something you struggle with, remember – it's not your fault! Modern society has been arranged to promote self-consciousness, which just means that being able to lose it will require more intention and effort. It also underscores the importance of flow in modern culture, the elusive feeling when we are not aware of scrutinizing the self in any way. "Because enjoyable activities have clear goals, stable rules, and challenges well matched to skills, there is little opportunity for the self to be threatened" (Csikszentmihalyi 1990, p. 63).

A common misconception of flow, however, is that these experiences mean we have completely "let go" of all awareness of our bodies and minds. On the contrary, we are completely aware of every movement our body or is making or thoughts crossing our minds when in the midst of a flow activity, but every ounce of these movements and thoughts are going towards the activity itself.

> *A violinist must be extremely aware of every movement of her fingers, as well as of the sound entering her ears, and of the total form of the piece she is playing, both analytically, note by note, and holistically, in terms of its overall design…so loss of self-consciousness does not involve a loss of self, and certainly not a loss of consciousness, but rather, only a loss of consciousness* of *the self.*
>
> *(Csikszentmihalyi 1990, p. 64)*

Once a person emerges from a flow experience and is able to reflect on it, she will mostly feel a deep sense of gratification, having just completed an activity that was not only enjoyable, but allowed her to gain new skills and expand the self.

Sense of Control

When in the midst of a flow experience, we feel a sense of control over our actions and can instinctively react to what comes next during the task (Nakamura and Csikszentmihalyi 2002, 2009). What is interesting, however, is that this sense of control is not necessarily the same as actual control. For example, a basketball player may miss a shot, or the accountant may input the wrong number while experiencing flow. Nevertheless, the individual perceives that he is in control throughout the flow activity and does not fear losing control like we often do in daily life.

As a chess player explains, "...I have a general feeling of well-being, and that I am in complete control of my world" (Csikszentmihalyi 1990, p. 60). Although control is perceived, our sense of actual control over a flow activity grows considerably as we build our skills. For example, a public speaker who continues to practice her skills will gain more and more control over the subject material over time and be less likely to make an error during a speech. Those moments where we feel like "I've got this" are when we become aware of that sense of control.

The pace of modern life, where every email is expected to have an immediate reply and technological changes cause a constant feeling of instability, have caused many of us to feel more out of control over the outcomes of our lives than in previous eras. So many of the circumstances that impact the human experience – technology, the economy, the environment, the political climate, to name a few – seem to be largely out of our immediate control on a daily basis. This feeling can cause a sense of dejection and fatigue, where finding the effort to engage in a flow activity may feel more difficult. However, it is precisely because of this feeling that pursuing the activities that allow us to feel control and enjoyment are more vital than ever.

Losing Track of Time

As former NBA player Ben Gordon mentioned when describing his experience of being "in the zone," we lose track of time during the flow task. In most cases, time seems to move much faster than usual, with hours passing in what feels like minutes. The activity itself has its own rhythm and mechanisms to convey progress that usually do not conform to a specific time sequence. For example, when a doctor experiences flow while performing a surgery, she has a clear goal, mechanisms for feedback, and feels total involvement in the task.

With these flow parameters in place, it is likely she will lose track of time during the surgery, and she will know when the surgery is complete without the assistance of a clock. Here is how a ballet dancer describes the experience: "Two things happen. One is that it seems to pass really fast in one sense. After it's passed, it seems to have passed really fast. I see that it's 1:00 in the morning, and I say: 'Aha, just a few minutes ago it was 8:00'" (Csikszentmihalyi 1990, p. 66). The fastest man alive, gold medalist Usain Bolt, says that time would feel like it slowed down when in the midst of a sprint. When someone returns from vacation and we ask them how their time was, we'll often hear, "It flew by!" as a response. We tend to be more present and less distracted on vacation, which contributes to our sense of time moving at a different cadence than when in the midst of our daily lives. Yes, while we all would love to make time slow down while doing something we love, it's somewhat of a paradox – becoming too aware of time passing will take us out of flow.

So much of daily life, more than we realize, is guided by the clock. Take a typical day of a working parent: Alarm clock to wake up at 6:30 am, drop kids at school by 8 am, be at work by 9 am, meetings at 10, 12, 2, and 3 pm, pick up kids by 5 pm, dinner at 6 pm, bedtime at 8 pm. The clock provides the structure for society to run smoothly and for families, businesses, and communities to function. A constant awareness of the time, however, is its own form of concentration that is not inherently enjoyable, and thus not flow conducive. Flow activities tend to be the only time in a day where our pace and progress are not guided by a clock, and the mechanisms of the activity offer their own intervals that mark the transition from one stage to the next.

Intrinsic Motivation

While the above components are key aspects of the flow experience, a vital condition for one to experience flow in any capacity is that she is intrinsically motivated to pursue the flow activity (Abuhamdeh and Csikszentmihalyi 2009; Csikszentmihalyi 1975, 1990; Csikszentmihalyi and Rathunde 1993; Nakamura and Csikszentmihalyi 2002). Intrinsic motivation is conceptualized by the psychologists Ryan and Deci (2000) as taking part in something because one inherently enjoys it or finds it interesting. In contrast, extrinsic motivation refers to taking part in something because of the external reward or outcome that it provides. For example, some individuals may be motivated to perform in their jobs because they love their work (intrinsic motivation), while others may be motivated by the money and lifestyle it affords them (extrinsic motivation). In the context of flow, one pursues the flow task for its own sake because of the optimal experience it provides – simply being able to take part in the task is the reward. In other words, flow is an experience that is worth pursuing even without the presence of an external reward.

Some activities may originally be pursued for the external reward they provide, only to become intrinsically rewarding over time. For example, an individual may initially pursue a career as a lawyer because of the potential salary, and eventually may find she loves learning about and practicing law, thus turning aspects of her job into a flow experience. Sure, in the context of leisure activities and hobbies, it's easy to be intrinsically motivated. But what about work? We all need to work and earn money, which is an extrinsic reward. However, our work can also provide so much else that contributes to us becoming the best version of ourselves, which creates intrinsic rewards – for example, challenge, growth, and connection. When we think about what a "great job" looks like, money will not be the only thing on that list. It's that other stuff that creates the opportunity for flow in our professional lives.

When an activity is intrinsically motivating, it is an autotelic experience, derived from two Greek words (*auto* meaning self, *telos* meaning goal). The experience itself is the reward. As a surgeon describes it: "It is so enjoyable that I would do it even if I didn't have to" (Csikszentmihalyi 1990, p. 67). The opposite of autotelic is exotelic, an activity done for external reasons only. If we consider autotelic and exotelic to be two ends of a spectrum, most activities we pursue fall somewhere in between. Activities aren't static either: What could start as fully autotelic, playing basketball for instance, could then become exotelic if that person become skilled enough to play professionally. In the example of the lawyer above, what may have started as a purely exotelic career choice to practice law – done for money, status, and prestige – may then become somewhat autotelic over time if aspects of the job become enjoyable and gratifying. Any professional activity will have an exotelic element, but if a job is purely exotelic, it will cease to be particularly energizing and enjoyable. If a job is purely autotelic, it may not provide enough exotelic reward to be able to afford basic needs and support a family. Therefore, exotelic endeavors may afford us the time and money to pursue leisure activities that are autotelic. There is no perfect formula, but our lives should find a healthy balance between both ends of this spectrum.

Flow in Modern Society

The nine dimensions of flow that Mihaly identified (Nakamura and Csikszentmihalyi 2002) still hold up remarkably well decades later – a testament to his enduring legacy. Research in the last three decades has confirmed the positive benefits of the flow experience, leading to higher levels of well-being (Haworth 1993), self-concept (Jackson et al. 2001), performance (Harris et al. 2023; Jackson and Roberts 1992), and creativity (Zubair and Kamal 2015).

What has changed the most is the shifting context of where flow experiences now take place – the core differences being the amount of attention we now invest in the digital world, not only impacting where flow is found in general but also fundamentally changing how and where we work. For example, I may be intrinsically motivated by working from home – an option that largely did not exist during early formulations of the flow theory. Or I may find flow while creating presentations in PowerPoint or writing code. In the leisure context, I may find deep immersion going on internet "deep dives" on certain subjects that can consume hours of an evening in what feels like 10 minutes. More recently, the rise of AI has created a whole new domain for potential flow experiences, which will continue to evolve at a frighteningly rapid pace; we will cover this in more depth later in the book. Studies have indicated that flow does indeed exist in the world of digital media (Cowley et al. 2008) and even when using Facebook (Mauri et al. 2011).

When finding flow in new contexts, it also means we must be more intentional in abiding by flow's characteristics. Having a clear goal, for example, may take more time and thought when engaging in a digital task that we have less experience with, or the sources of feedback may not be as apparent. Flow's landmines have also increased, as alluded to with the time confetti concept at the beginning of the chapter. For as much potential for flow as the digital world holds, businesses devote millions of dollars to try and pry our attention away from what we are doing and toward their product or service. If we are not careful, the default way of living will be to be perpetually out of flow, popcorning our attention every minute or two until bed, only to wake up and do it over again.

Optimal experience depends on a level of intentionality that was not necessary in the twentieth century, when it was easier to devote our attention to one thing because there wasn't the choice of thousands of other activities at our fingertips. Think of it like aisles of a grocery store – there are twice as many healthy food (flow) aisles as there once were, but there are 10 times as many junk food aisles. Without the intention to purchase from the healthy aisles, it is far too easy to be drawn to, and get lost in, the junk food aisles.

Mihaly (1975, 2000) suggested that not all personality types are equally prone to experiencing flow. While it is indeed a universal experience, there are differences in the frequency and intensity of flow for different individuals. He suggests that individuals with an autotelic personality are more likely to experience and stay in flow. Individuals with this type of personality are more likely to pursue activities for their own sake and tend to be naturally curious with a low level of self-centeredness. This natural wonder about the world enables these individuals to seek opportunities to build their skills and pursue substantial challenges, and they are able to endure and persist throughout the experience (Baumann 2012; Ullen et al. 2012). While autotelic personality has been found to be partially inherited genetically, environmental factors play a notable role as well (Gosling et al. 2012)

The natural pursuit of flow in the digital realm will likely result in *microflow,* when some of flow's characteristics are present and the task is engaging but has a low level of complexity (Csikszentmihalyi 1975). This is in contrast to macroflow, or a core flow experience, a more complex, all-encompassing experience where all of flow's characteristics are present and the self expands as a result. Microflow is now instantly accessible, where we can instantly engage our minds by playing an online game when in line at Starbucks. The ease with which we can access microflow experiences may inhibit the autotelic desire to pursue more macroflow experiences. Back to the food analogy, it is much easier to pick up fast food than it is to prepare a meal of protein, complex carbs, and vegetables. Modern society is much friendlier to the pursuit of microflow, and unwittingly frowns upon macroflow experiences. In a complex macroflow experience, we are no longer instantly available since we are immersed in the flow task, meaning we wouldn't instantly reply to a text or email, or check every digital notification as it arrives. This could lead to frustration from our family, friends, and coworkers, and could cause them to see us as less reliable and communicative. Therefore, we should not only make room in our lives for macroflow experiences ourselves but also encourage these types of experiences for others in our lives, showing grace if they don't immediately respond and asking questions about the aspects of their lives that bring energy and joy.

It is also imperative that we encourage our youth to engage in macroflow activities and provide the environment for autotelic personalities to blossom, for the intrinsic pursuit of flow experiences at a young age will be more likely to translate into adulthood. A diet of only macroflow experiences is unrealistic and ultimately unhealthy for our personal and professional relationships, but our ability to fully realize the self, becoming who we are meant to be, depends on carving out time for holistic, macroflow experiences and not slipping into a lifetime of transitory microflow.

References

Abuhamdeh, S. and Csikszentmihalyi, M. (2009). Intrinsic and extrinsic motivational orientations in the competitive context: An examination of person–situation interactions. *Journal of Personality* 77(5): 1615–1635.

Baumann, N. (2012). Autotelic personality. In S. Engeser (ed.), *Advances in Flow Research* (pp. 165–186). Springer Science + Business Media.

Cowley, B., Charles, D., Black, M., and Hickey, R. (2008). Towards an understanding of flow in video games. *Computers in Entertainment* 6(2): 1–27.

Csikszentmihalyi, M. (1975). *Beyond boredom and anxiety*. San Francisco: Jossey-Bass.

Csikszentmihalyi, M. (1985). Emergent motivation and the evolution of the self. *Advances in Motivation and Achievement* 4: 93–119.

Csikszentmihalyi, M. (1990). *Flow: The Psychology of Optimal Experience*. New York: HarperCollins.

Csikszentmihalyi, M. (1997). *Finding Flow: The Psychology of Engagement with Everyday Life*. New York: HarperCollins.

Csikszentmihalyi, M. (2003). *Good Business: Leadership, Flow, and the Making of Meaning*. New York: Viking.

Csikszentmihalyi, M. and Csikszentmihalyi, I. S. (eds.) (1988). *Optimal Experience: Psychological Studies of Flow in Consciousness*. New York: Cambridge University Press.

Csikszentmihalyi, M. and Rathunde, K. (1993). The measurement of flow in everyday life: Toward a theory of emergent motivation. *Nebraska Symposium on Motivation* 40: 57–97.

Davies, H. (1996). *The Beatles* (2nd rev. ed.). W. W. Norton.

Earls, J. (2007). *How to Become a Guitar Player from Hell*. Fritch, TX: Peroma Publications.

Gosling, J., Jones, S., and Sutherland, I. (2012). *Key Concepts in Leadership*. SAGE Publications Ltd.

Harris, D. J., Allen, K. L., Vine, S. J., and Wilson, M. R. (2023). A systematic review and meta-analysis of the relationship between flow states and performance. *International Review of Sport and Exercise Psychology* 16(1): 693–721.

Haworth, J. T. (1993). Skill-challenge relationships and psychological well-being in everyday life. *Society and Leisure* 16(1): 115–128.

Jackson, S. A. and Roberts, G. C. (1992). Positive performance states of athletes: Toward a conceptual understanding of peak performance. *The Sports Psychologist* 6(2): 156–171.

Jackson, S. A., Thomas, P. R., Marsh, H. W., and Smethurst, C. J. (2001). Relationships between flow, self-concept, psychological skills, and performance. *Journal of Applied Sport Psychology* 13(2): 129–153.

Kennedy, K. (ed.). (2005, February 21). Players. *Sports Illustrated*, pp. 29–35.

Mauri, M., Cipresso, P., Balgera, A., and Villamira, M. (2011). Why is Facebook so successful? Psychophysiological measures describe a core flow state while using Facebook. *Cyberpsychology and Behavior: The Impact of the Internet, Multimedia, and Virtual Reality on Behavior and Society* 14(12): 723–731.

Microsoft. (2023, May 9). *Will AI fix work?* WorkLab. Retrieved from https://www.microsoft.com/en-us/worklab/work-trend-index/will-ai-fix-work

Nakamura, J. and Csikszentmihalyi, M. (2002). The concept of flow. In C. R. Snyder and S. J. Lopez (eds.), *Handbook of Positive Psychology* (pp. 89–105). New York: Oxford University Press.

Nakamura, J. and Csikszentmihalyi, M. (2009). Flow theory and research. In S. J. Lopez and C. R. Snyder (eds.), *Oxford Handbook of Positive Psychology* (3rd ed., pp. 195–206). New York: Oxford University Press.

Nakamura, J. and Dubin, M. (2015). Flow in motivational psychology. In J.D. Wright (ed.), *International Encyclopedia of the Social and Behavioral Sciences* (2nd ed., pp. 260–265). Waltham, MA: Elsevier.

Peterson, C. (2006). *A Primer in Positive Psychology*. New York, NY: Oxford University Press.

Publisher (2015, May 19). *Sodajerker presents... Adam Duritz. Songwriting Magazine*. Retrieved from https://www.songwritingmagazine.co.uk/interviews/sodajerker-presents-adam-duritz

Ryan, R. M. and Deci, E. L. (2000). Intrinsic and extrinsic motivations: Classic definitions and new directions. *Contemporary Educational Psychology*, 25: 54–67.

Saefong, B. (2021, August 6). *5 songs guitarists need to hear by...Jimi Hendrix*. Retrieved from https://www.musicradar.com/news/5-songs-guitarists-need-to-hear-by-jimi-hendrix

Saymeh, A. (2023, February 22). *What is imposter syndrome? Definition, symptoms, and overcoming it.* BetterUp. Retrieved from https://www.betterup.com/blog/what-is-imposter-syndrome-and-how-to-avoidit#:~:text=Imposter%20syndrome%20is%20the%20condition,phony%22%20and%20doubting%20their%20abilities

Schulte, B. (2020, October 7). *Time confetti and the broken promise of leisure.* Retrieved from https://www.newamerica.org/better-life-lab/in-the-news/time-confetti-and-broken-promise-leisure/

Shelton, R. (1978, July 29). *Expecting rain.* Retrieved from https://www.expectingrain.com/dok/int/shelton1978.07.29.html

Uitti, J. (2022). *The top 22 Jimi Hendrix quotes.* American songwriter. Retrieved from https://americansongwriter.com/the-top-22-jimi-hendrix-quotes/

Ullen, F., Manzano, O., Almeida, A., Magnusson, P. K. E., Pedersen, N. L., Csikszentmihalyi, M., and Madison, G. (2012). Proneness for psychological flow in everyday life: Associations with personality and intelligence. *Personality and Individual Differences* 52: 167–172.

Zubair, A. and Kamal, A. (2015). Authentic leadership and creativity: Mediating role of work-related flow and psychological capital. *Journal of Behavioural Sciences* 25(1): 150–171.

3

Flowing Together

An Overview of Collective Flow

"Other People Matter." When I (Dubin) sat down for the first lecture of a Positive Psychology course at the University of Michigan in 2008 with Dr. Christopher Peterson, these were the first three words he uttered. He said if you could boil the research of Positive Psychology down to three words, the single factor that most consistently predicts satisfaction, well-being, and happiness is the quality of our relationships. Of course, there are thousands of relationships we will have in our lives: Family, friends, classmates, teammates, teachers, coaches, professors, roommates, bosses, co-workers, the list goes on and on. All of these relationships can serve as a profoundly meaningful source of flow, and a source of overall meaning in our lives. When relational goals are misaligned, they can also serve as the source of debilitating stress and anxiety, causing chaos and psychic entropy. The early research on flow conducted by Mihaly and his colleagues focused on flow as an individual experience, but Mihaly was quite aware of the impact of other people on our lives. "It is not surprising that in our studies of the quality of daily experience it has been demonstrated again and again that people report the most positive moods overall when they are with friends" (Csikszentmihalyi 1990, p. 186). He focused on our relationships with family, friends, and the wider community, and how the conditions for experiencing flow as individuals (goals, feedback, skill/challenge balance) still applied in these relationships. For example, here is how he discussed immediate goals in the context of family: "As with any other flow activity, family activities should also provide clear

Flow 2.0: Optimal Experience in a Complex World. Honoring Mihaly Csikszentmihalyi's Legacy, First Edition. Stewart I. Donaldson and Matthew Dubin.
© 2025 John Wiley & Sons Ltd. Published 2025 by John Wiley & Sons Ltd.

feedback. In this case, it is simply a matter of keeping open channels of communication. If a husband does not know what bothers his wife, and vice versa, neither has the opportunity to reduce the inevitable tensions that will arise" (Csikszentmihalyi 1990, p. 181). In the years since, more attention has been paid on group flow as it pertains to groups of people who come together for the reason of accomplishing goals and performing at a high level: sports teams, work teams, music groups, etc.

The power of flow can help us bring out the best in ourselves, but our true potential as human beings lies in the collective. When a team is performing at the peak of its powers, each member is individually in flow, but our individual flow is completely reliant on the actions of our teammates. Phil Jackson, who won a record 11 NBA championships as a coach and knows a bit about coaching players into individual flow (Michael Jordan and Kobe Bryant) and teams into collective flow (the Chicago Bulls and LA Lakers), says: "The strength of the team is each individual member. The strength of each member is the team" (as cited in Wyatt 2021).

Terms to Describe Flow with Others

Several terms have risen to describe the experience of flow with others, including social flow and group flow (Pels et al. 2018). Our personal favorite term to describe the experience is collective flow. The word *collective* is defined by the Cambridge Dictionary as "of or shared by every member of a group of people," which wonderfully encapsulates what it means to be in this state of flow with others: Each person shares in the experience and owns a piece of what a group is able to accomplish together. Throughout the rest of the chapter, we will be referring to flow with other people as "collective flow."

Collective flow is the experience of flow occurring between two or more individuals who are partially dependent on each other's actions and behaviors. In 2010, Walker identified three types of flow experiences. The first is *individual solitary* flow, which is the experience of flow that occurs completely on our own. This could be playing the guitar, baking, lifting weights — anything where flow occurs when no other people are present, the flow most commonly explored in Mihaly's original research and writings.

The next type of flow Walker identified is *coactive social* flow. This is when we are in flow with other people present, but we aren't directly interacting/collaborating with the other people around. For example, let's say we go on a jog with friends – we are doing the same activity together, but don't need to directly interact to find flow while doing it. Another common example of this is shared workspaces, where individuals get their work done in the company of others, although each person is working on different things. For those who thrive in these types of spaces, they often derive energy and focus from the presence of others, even if not in direct interaction with them. Going to a movie theater or concert can also be a rich source of coactive social flow, providing a sometimes-cathartic communal experience.

The last type of flow is *interactive social* flow. This is the most collaborative type of flow and is most heavily reliant on others. For example, let's say we're playing in a band or playing on a basketball team. Our ability to find flow with our band members or teammates heavily relies on their personality, behaviors, and actions, and their ability to find flow relies on us. In Walker's (2010) research, he found that college students reported flow with others to be more enjoyable than solitary flow – another finding that backs Peterson's (2006) ethos: Other People Matter.

Take two people having a conversation about a topic they are each passionate about. In fact, Mihaly identified that the most common place people experienced flow was in conversation with others. Let's say these two people are huge fans of the Netflix TV show *Stranger Things* and are exploring potential theories of what is going to happen in the final season. They both are equally knowledgeable about the story and the characters and therefore can have an in-depth conversation about the show that enables them both to experience flow while discussing it. However, let's say two people try to have a conversation about the show where one person is a huge fan and the other has never seen it. The discrepancy in knowledge and passion about the show between the two individuals will make it much more difficult for the conversation to progress to a level that enables them both to experience flow.

Ten Factors for Creating Collective Flow

Now let's take a group of people that are ideating and brainstorming new ideas. For example, the writers of *Stranger Things* who are mapping out the plot for the final season. Adding more individuals to the setting facilitates complexity. Creating an environment where all of the individuals in the room can experience flow together to create the most creative, intricate, high-quality story depends on a myriad of factors. Let's explore what those factors are, where they overlap with individual flow, and where they differ. To explore this, I will be referring to the factors identified by Keith Sawyer, a former student of Mihaly who studied jazz ensembles, improv groups, and business professionals, and author of *Group Genius: The Creative Power of Collaboration* (2007). Sawyer identified 10 factors, as described here.

Group's Goal

To find flow on our own, we must be crystal clear on what we are trying to accomplish. In collective flow, we must share the same specific goal with the other people we're collaborating with, with no individual conflicting goals (Van den Hout et al. 2018). On a basketball team, the goal is clear during a game: Win the game by defeating the opponent. In work settings, sometimes the goal is more ambiguous, which can be a significant impediment to group flow. In a meeting, for example, what is the group trying to accomplish within the time allotted? Do they hope to come up with a new idea, or simply update each other on the status of existing projects?

Also, are we aware of how our individual goals contribute to the group's goal? Perhaps I know what we are trying to accomplish in a meeting, but I don't see how my role can meaningfully contribute to the group achieving its goal. On the basketball court, do I know where I'm supposed to stand on the court and how my actions directly contribute to the success of a particular sequence? If I'm the drummer in a band, the individual roles of the guitarists, singers, and keyboardists depend on me executing my role to near-perfection, keeping the beat on an agreed-upon rhythm that everyone else relies on.

While knowing what is meant to be accomplished in a meeting, a play on the court, or a particular song is more of a micro, short-term goal, organizations and teams can also facilitate a big picture shared vision that creates a consistent north star for each team to strive towards. For example, when the Beatles first became popular in the UK in 1962, Paul McCartney recalled setting a goal before going to the United States: "I'd said to Brian [Epstein, the band's manager], 'We don't want to go to America until we have a No. 1 record;" (as cited in

Tannenbaum 2015). So, while they had their micro goals of creating individual songs and performing live shows in the UK, they set a north star of needing a No. 1 record before they would tour on American soil. In late 1963, "I Want to Hold Your Hand" hit #1: "We were playing in Paris, an engagement at the Olympia Theatre, a famous old theater Edith Piaf played at, and we got a telegram – as you did in those days – saying, 'Congratulations, No. 1 in the US charts.' We jumped on each other's backs. It was late at night after a show, and we just partied" (Tannenbaum 2015). Several months later, they came to America and played their historic performance on the *Ed Sullivan Show* that was viewed by nearly half of the US population at the time: 73 million people (Figure 3.1).

The band had clear micro and macro goals that they all shared, keeping them focused amidst the chaos around them. Once the group's goal is clear, each individual can commit. As legendary NFL coach Vince Lombardi puts it, "Individual commitment to a group effort – that is what makes a team work, a company work, a society work, a civilization work" (as cited in 247 Sports).

Figure 3.1 The Beatles performing in front of 73 million people on the *Ed Sullivan Show* in 1964. *Source:* Associated Press / Alamy Stock Photo.

Close Listening

Many of us have been on a Zoom call where the other person is not fully locked in. We can tell their eyes are somewhere else, perhaps responding to an email or reading their latest iPhone notification. They may hear us, but are they really listening? For collective flow to occur, we must deeply listen to each other, and not just listen to respond. Listening takes effort and energy and is what makes or breaks the quality of our connections. How many times has someone started talking to us, where we have already mapped out how we are going to respond before they've finished talking? When we do this, we tune out the rest of what they have to say as we exert more of our energy remembering the content of our response.

Active listening (synonymous with close listening) consists of three components: cognitive, emotional, and behavioral (Jones et al. 2019 as cited in Abrahams and Groysberg 2021). The cognitive aspects of listening means we are fully attending to the explicit and implicit information we are receiving from the person speaking, ensuring we understand what we are hearing. The emotional aspect pertains to effectively managing our reactions during the conversation, remaining calm, exuding empathy, and avoiding the appearance of boredom, frustration, or annoyance. The behavioral component is showing verbal and nonverbal interest in the words being expressed so the other person feels heard and understood.

There are a myriad of strategies to practice the muscle of listening. One of our favorites includes listening with the intention of following up with a question. The art of coming up with a question forces us to focus our attention a little more thoughtfully on the content of the person talking to us, and our response is designed to have them elaborate and go deeper, thus giving us more opportunities to listen and learn from others. Another popular and effective strategy is to repeat the person's words back to them. This has two benefits: It helps us to digest and comprehend the content in a way where we feel comfortable verbally expressing it, and it makes the other person feel genuinely heard (Abrahams and Groysberg 2021).

Complete Concentration

While individual flow requires concentration on the task we are engaged with on our own, it's important that each individual is completely focused throughout the group activity for collective flow to occur. While we have more control over our own concentration in an individual flow task, ensuring the concentration of a pair or group of people is a more complex task. Perhaps one person is tired, another recently got in an argument with their spouse, and another is more introverted and gets overwhelmed in the presence of a group. Each person's individual circumstances and personality will impact their ability to concentrate in any given moment, even if other flow conditions are present.

In virtual settings – take a meeting conducted on Zoom, for example – one of the reasons collective flow is so challenging is because it is extremely difficult to fully concentrate. On Zoom, we can see ourselves in a little box on the screen, and we have everything the internet has to offer tempting us behind the Zoom window. The landmines that prevent full concentration are far more present in virtual meetings than in-person meetings (and flow in IRL meetings is hard enough). This is why it is essential to remove outside distractions when attempting to have a meaningful experience with another person or a group of people. Virtually, this is more challenging, since digital distractions are more difficult to remove when the digital device is necessary for the interaction.

These digital distractions available during a virtual meeting are like trying to avoid eating chips when there are 10 different types of chips in our pantry that we can easily grab. To successfully avoid eating chips, it would be far easier if they weren't right in front of us. In real-life interactions, avoiding these distractions is essential as well. For example, if a group of friends goes out to dinner and everyone places their phone on the table, it automatically draws attention to the stimuli our phones provide, taking attention away from each other, even if no one actively checks it. This creates a significant impediment to the group achieving flow together, since the interpersonal chemistry needed for flow to occur is complex enough without external distraction getting in the way.

Being in Control

To find flow in a group, we all must feel a sense of control over our own actions and how that contributes to the group's goals. Take a rock band, for example. Let's say one person is the lead singer, one person is the lead guitarist, one person is the keyboard player, and one person is the drummer. For group flow to occur, each band member has complete control and autonomy over their instrument and knows the role they play when they perform a song. Same with positions on a football team: The quarterback, running back, and wide receiver each have a set of distinct responsibilities and rely on each other to execute those responsibilities for the group to achieve its goal.

Many of us at work are not crystal clear on our roles and what we can and can't control, thus making collective flow difficult in many of our organizations. Like individual flow, this doesn't have to be *actual* control, but *perceived* control, where we feel subjective control over the situation in the moment. We may find out later that our actions needed to be modified in some way, like perhaps I shared the wrong data point in a presentation during a meeting, but in the midst of the moment itself, our control of the situation *feels* absolute.

Blending Egos

In individual flow, the ego falls away, allowing ourselves to completely devote our energy and attention to the flow task without any sense of self-consciousness. In collective flow, each ego must find a way to harmoniously coexist with the others in the group. Once this takes place, all of the egos can melt away together. So many toxic meetings share this attribute in common: People speaking up to make sure their voice is heard or to get ahead in a self-interested way, caring far more about their own performance in the meeting than helping the group reach a common goal. This type of behavior is contagious, and when one person does it, it often permeates and becomes a cultural norm.

We've also seen so many of the greatest partnerships fall apart at least partially due to clashes of ego, such as Lennon and McCartney, Roger Waters and David Gilmour, Simon and Garfunkel, and Shaquille O'Neal and Kobe Bryant. When a group shares a common goal, it is essential that each person's primary motivation is to defer self-interest in pursuit of the shared objective. One of flow's characteristics is the loss of self-consciousness, where we temporarily forget our own insecurities, anxieties, and any other self-centered thoughts that would take our attention away from the flow task.

When ego causes us to behave in a self-interested manner, it not only takes our attention away from the task, but it causes our teammates to not be able to find their flow since our actions are not reflecting the needs the task requires, but our own. Legendary UCLA basketball coach John Wooden put it best, as he often did: "A player who makes a team great is more valuable than a great player. Losing yourself in the group, for the good of the group – that's teamwork" (as cited in Gunderman 2019).

Equal Participation

For collective flow to occur, each person must have the skill set to actively participate. Not everyone has to have a perfectly equal role as far as the percentage that they are contributing to a group outcome, but a group should not include any extraneous participants who don't have a clearly defined way of adding value to the shared goal. For example, so many of our professional meetings are dominated by one person, with the other members acting as passive listeners. While these meetings can be necessary, these are not the type that facilitates collective flow. In contrast, a marketing team having a brainstorming meeting to come up with ideas for their new social media campaign, where each person in the meeting is expected to contribute their thoughts, is far more likely to foster the type of engagement that leads to collective flow. Successful participation also requires a keen awareness of each person's strengths to know where they can best contribute to the group's goal. In a band, for example, the guitarist and drummer would focus on their respective instruments because that's what they do – we wouldn't have the guitarist switch to drums and the drummer switch to guitar at the last minute before a concert. In other group settings, it can be more of a challenge to fall into a natural role where we know how we will best contribute.

Take a brainstorm meeting in a work setting. Often, when individual group members are unsure how to participate, they will defer to the highest-ranking person in the room. These types of politics are difficult to ignore when we are *not* in flow – we will be keenly aware of the pecking order in any situation we walk into. However, if we had a clear mode of participation going into that meeting (e.g., I am the customer service expert and am expected to contribute when we are discussing how to best meet the needs of our customers), our focus can then begin to shift away from interpersonal dynamics, egos, and politics and towards the shared group goal.

Familiarity

We are much more likely to find collective flow when we share tacit knowledge with our collaborators. Tacit knowledge refers to a set of unspoken understandings and assumptions that we have with others that often come when we have collaborated with them for a substantial period of time. When we know how people tick, what energizes them, what their pet peeves are, and how they prefer to think and communicate, we can "play off them," so to speak, and have a shorthand way of interacting with each other. For example, let's say an extrovert and an introvert are working together. They may share an understanding that the extrovert is going to think out loud, while the introvert is going to write down more notes and take a little more time to gather their thoughts before sharing their ideas. The introvert may prefer to see a meeting agenda in advance, for example, to have time to reflect and prepare beforehand, enabling them to best contribute when called upon. If each person knows this about the other, they can expect certain types of behaviors and contributions almost subconsciously, allowing them to stay immersed in the flow task.

When we bring on new team members, it often takes some time before we can find flow with them. This is why it's so important to learn what makes them tick and what their motivators are early on in the relationship, to accelerate the path toward familiarity. On a deeper level, a sense of familiarity eventually will allow us to read people's nonverbal cues – picking up on their emotions such as enthusiasm, frustration, and fatigue without any associated words. We can then adjust our own behavior accordingly, enhancing the possibility that we can remain immersed in a shared task by managing not only our own emotions but also the emotions of our fellow group members.

Communication

Groups that successfully find flow together are constantly communicating. The kind of communication that facilitates collective flow is often spontaneous conversation that defers ego and enables all participants to get in on the action in a meaningful way. Unplanned communication stems from authentically listening to those we are interacting with, our responses predicated on what is heard. Communication is how knowledge is shared, both the explicit kind (which is more objective) and also tacit knowledge – a more subjective form of information that is picked up from observation, imitation, and consistent interactions over time (Koskinen et al. 2003; Nonaka and Takeuchi 1995; Van den Hout et al. 2018).

At work, communication facilitates the key preconditions to experiencing individual flow: Having a clear goal, immediate feedback, and the balance between challenge and skill. Managers should communicate with their people to define goals, give frequent feedback that is specific and actionable, and support their people in making sure the challenges of their people's work don't exceed or undersell their skillset. Beyond verbal communication, nonverbal communication will also facilitate a collective flow experience – a key element of tacit knowledge.

One of the great management thinkers of our time, Peter Drucker, said, "The most important thing in communication is to hear what isn't being said" (Drucker 2016). As mentioned above, we must be deeply familiar with our fellow group members to be able communicate nonverbally, read between the lines, and support each other to ensure we don't lose focus on the collective flow task.

Keep it Moving Forward

Sawyer uses the improv technique, "Yes and..." as an example here. In an improv scene, when one person establishes the parameters of a situation (e.g., they are in a coffee shop and are ordering 12 coffees that they are going to drink throughout the week), it is the responsibility of their partner in the scene to deeply listen, accept what they've said, and build on it. If their response was, "That's a terrible idea and makes no sense, we're actually in a gym lifting weights," it would stop the scene in its tracks and completely impede the ability to find collective flow. The scene partner would willingly accept the parameters of the scene and build on it to flesh it out.

At work, we often do not utilize the "yes and" technique, even if our intentions are in the right place. For example, if we disagree with someone's idea, it is important that we be able to express our opinion without fear of repercussion. However, it is important that we disagree with someone in a way that still acknowledges what they said and how it is contributing to the overall discussion. Being able to take risks and speak our minds without fear of repercussion is the core tenet of psychological safety (Edmonson and Lei 2014), a core component of successful collaboration toward a shared outcome.

In 2012, Google embarked on a study (Duhigg 2016) to identify the factors most essential to building a high-performing team. They called this Project Aristotle, where they studied hundreds of Google's teams to decipher why some were more effective than others. Julia Rozovsky, a researcher who was hired by Google to work on Project Aristotle, remembered having very unfulfilling meetings with her Yale business school classmates in their study group, battling for idea supremacy and

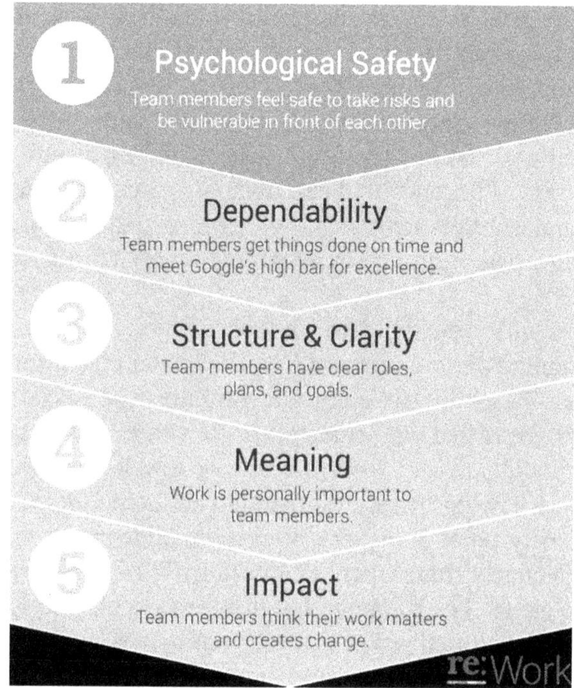

Figure 3.2 Top five factors in a high-performing team. *Source:* https://rework.withgoogle.com/jp/guides/understanding-team-effectiveness#help-teams-determine-their-needs/GoogleLLC/last accessed April 02, 2024.

who would get to present in class: "I always felt like I had to prove myself...people would try to show authority by speaking louder or talking over each other. I always felt like I had to be careful not to make mistakes around them" (Duhigg 2016). The work of Rozovsky and team on Project Aristotle found that psychological safety was the number one factor that led to a high performing team – essentially the opposite experience that Rozovsky had in her business school study group. See the five top factors that Project Aristotle identified in Figure 3.2.

Patrick Lencioni (2002), the author of the classic book *The 5 Dysfunctions of a Team*, seconds this notion: "Teamwork begins by building trust. And the only way to do that is to overcome our need for invulnerability."

The Potential for Failure

To find collective flow, the group needs to feel a sense of shared stakes. These stakes aren't meant to stoke fear, but rather provide structure of how to operate, what success looks like, and what failure looks like.

When we set a collective goal, not wanting to "fail" creates a sense of urgency that galvanizes a group to focus together. Sometimes, collective goals are time bound, enabling us to know what success or failure looks like (e.g., outscore your opponent in 60 minutes of game time, reach a revenue target by the end of the fiscal year). Creating a time-bound goal creates a sense of urgency that can maximize focus. As the legendary composer Leonard Bernstein said, "To achieve great things, two things are needed; a plan, and not quite enough time" (*Reader's Digest* 2006) (Figure 3.3).

Sometimes other rules will apply that let us know whether we're successful (e.g., the client signing off on a proposal, a Michelin Star review for a fine-dining restaurant). Personally, we enjoy playing tennis and basketball and consider them to be two of our primary flow activities. However, if we're not playing competitively and keeping score, we find it basically impossible to find flow. Knowing there is a possibility of losing creates heightened stakes for every point and every possession, allowing us to lock in much more effectively than when simply rallying or shooting around. Ultimately, the game doesn't matter, but in the moment, it feels like it matters because we've created stakes that everyone agrees to.

Figure 3.3 Conductor Leonard Bernstein at the climax of Mahler's Resurrection symphony performed by the Boston Symphony in Lenox, Massachusetts. *Source:* Bettmann/Getty Images.

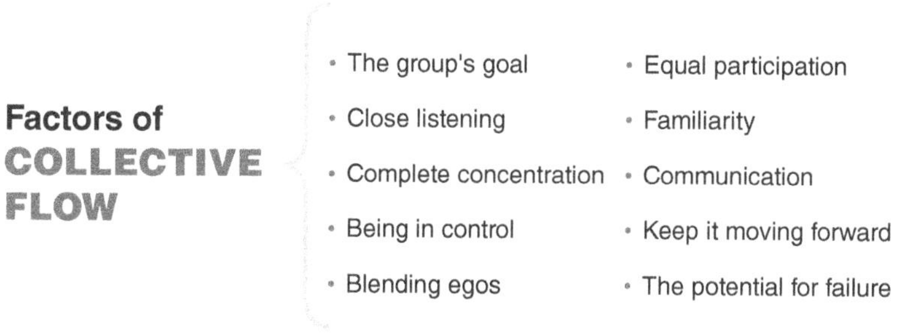

Factors of COLLECTIVE FLOW

- The group's goal
- Close listening
- Complete concentration
- Being in control
- Blending egos
- Equal participation
- Familiarity
- Communication
- Keep it moving forward
- The potential for failure

Figure 3.4 Factors of collective flow.

Collective flow works similarly (Figure 3.4). As Sawyer notes, it is difficult for a jazz group to find flow during rehearsal, but during a live performance with an audience, where they can't be sure that the show will be successful, they are able to find a zone together that can be truly magical. At work, it is important we understand the stakes of what we're working on and why it matters to the success of our team and company. We don't need to have the most exciting role every day, but we should at least know how it's adding value, creating higher stakes and the potential for failure. Also, the ability to come up with creative ideas is flow-conducive because it stretches our skills and creates a potential for failure.

The Power of Collective Flow

Adding these factors together can create various tensions that may seem paradoxical, but actually are facilitating the collective flow experience. As Sawyer says, "Group flow happens when many tensions are in perfect balance: the tension between convention and novelty, between structure and improvisation, between the critical, analytic mind and the freewheeling, outside-the-box mind, between listening to the rest of the group and speaking out with your own individual voice."

Our ability to find group flow is going to depend on a myriad of individual factors that aren't necessarily reflected in the list above: Our energy and mood on a particular day, whether we are collaborating in-person or remotely, whether our personality meshes with our teammates in an effective way, etc. Collective flow is more complex than individual flow because there is not only the individual's relationship with the task at hand but the individual's relationship with all of the other members of the group. This can make group flow hard to come by unless each person is fully present, committed to the shared goal and deferring self-interest.

One of the findings from Dubin's (2018) dissertation is that flow is contagious. The energy, effort, and mindset that each member brings to a conversation, project, activity, or game has a profound effect on the emotional and cognitive state of the other members of the group. This is similar to the emotional contagion theory, which asserts that we all tend to innately mimic each other's facial expressions, postures, and emotions, creating synchrony with each other (Bavelas et al. 1987; Hatfield et al. 1993). If one member of a virtual work meeting is distracted and clearly focused on other things, the other members of the meeting are more like to be distracted and multitask. If one person has their camera on and one has their camera off, that will create an incongruous environment that would inhibit the ability for the group to find flow and achieve emotional synchronicity.

However, the power of the collective can create the most euphoric, magical flow that exists. When a group feels a sense of collective efficacy, where the group has a shared belief in their joint power to achieve a common goal, flow ensues (Salanova et al. 2014). Think of collective flow as a higher-risk, higher-reward proposition – it may be harder to come by than individual flow, but when it happens, what we are able to accomplish far exceeds what any of us could do on our own. When we find a group that we can experience flow with, we must take special care to maintain the relationships that help to facilitate these shared experiences. Collective flow requires a level of trust with the fellow members of our group, where we can completely give ourselves over to the needs of the collective without fear that we may say the wrong thing or have a dumb idea. We don't need to be best friends with our group members, but we must have an understanding of one another and a clear idea of how our skill set and role mesh with and complement theirs. The greatest achievements in human history, those that awe and inspire us, are largely created by groups, not individuals.

References

Abrahams, R. and Groysberg, B. (2021, December 21). How to become a better listener. *Harvard Business Review*. https://hbr.org/2021/12/how-to-become-a-better-listener

Associated Press. (2024, February 9). Today in history: The Beatles appear on "The Ed Sullivan Show." *Chicago Tribune*. https://www.chicagotribune.com/2024/02/09/today-in-history-the-beatles-appear-on-the-ed-sullivan-show/

Bavelas, J. B., Black, A., Lemery, C. R., and Mullett, J. (1987). Motor mimicry as primitive empathy. In N. Eisenberg and J. Strayer (eds.), *Empathy and Its Development* (pp. 317–338). Cambridge University Press.

Cambridge Dictionary. Retrieved from https://dictionary.cambridge.org/us/dictionary/english/collective

Csikszentmihalyi, M. (1990). *Flow: The Psychology of Optimal Experience*. New York: HarperCollins.

Drucker, P. (2016). In S. Ratcliffe (ed.), *Oxford Essential Quotations*. Oxford University Press.

Dubin, M. (2018). Experiencing flow at work as a digital native in an accelerated knowledge economy. Doctoral dissertation. Claremont Graduate University, Claremont, CA.

Duhigg, C. (2016, February 25). *What Google Learned from Its Quest to Build the Perfect Team. The New York Times Magazine*. https://www.nytimes.com/2016/02/28 /magazine/what-google-learned-from-its-quest-to-build-the-perfect-team.html

Edmondson, A. C. and Lei, Z. (2014). Psychological safety: The history, renaissance, and future of an interpersonal construct. *Annual Review of Organizational Psychology and Organizational Behavior* 1: 23–43.

Gunderman, R. (2019, May 16). Life lessons of the greatest coach. *Psychology Today*. https://www.psychologytoday.com/us/blog/fully-human/201905/life-lessons-the-greatest-coach

Hatfield, E., Cacioppo, J. T., and Rapson, R. L. (1993). Emotional contagion. *Current Directions in Psychological Science* 2(3): 96–99.

Jones, S. M., Bodie, G. D., and Hughes, S. D. (2019). The impact of mindfulness on empathy, active listening, and perceived provisions of emotional support. *Communication Research* 46(6): 838–865.

Koskinen, K. U., Pihlanto, P., and Vanharanta, H. (2003). Tacit knowledge acquisition and sharing in a project work context. *International Journal of Project Management* 21(4): 281–290.

Lencioni, P. (2002). *The 5 Dysfunctions of a Team*. San Francisco, CA: Jossey-Bass.

Nonaka, I. and Takeuchi, H. (1995). *The Knowledge-Creating Company: How Japanese Companies Create the Dynamics of Innovation*. Oxford, UK: Oxford University Press.

Pels, F., Kleinert, J., and Mennigen, F. (2018). Group flow: A scoping review of definitions, theoretical approaches, measures and findings. *PLoS ONE* 13(12).

Peterson, C. (2006). *A Primer in Positive Psychology*. New York: Oxford University Press.

Peterson, C. (2008, June 17). Other people matter: Two examples. *Psychology Today*. https://www.psychologytoday.com/us/blog/the-good-life/200806/other-people-matter-two-examples

Reader's Digest. (2006). *Treasury of Wit and Wisdom: 4,000 of the Funniest, Cleverest, Most Insightful Things Ever Said*. Reader's Digest Association.

Salanova, M., Rodríguez-Sánchez, A. M., Schaufeli, W. B., and Cifre, E. (2014). Flowing together: A longitudinal study of collective efficacy and collective flow among workgroups. *The Journal of Psychology: Interdisciplinary and Applied*, *148*(4), 435–455.

Sawyer, K. (2007). *Group Genius: The Creative Power of Collaboration*. Basic Books.

Tannebaum, R. (2015, November 12). Billboard cover: Paul McCartney reveals the stories behind the Beatles' no. 1 hits. *Billboard*. https://www.billboard.com/music/music-news/billboard-cover-paul-mccartney-on-beatles-number-one-hits-6760851/

Understand "What is an effective team?" Google re:Work. https://rework.withgoogle.com/jp/guides/understanding-team-effectiveness#introduction

Van den Hout, J. J. J., Davis, O. C., and Weggeman, M. C. D. P. (2018). The conceptualization of team flow. *The Journal of Psychology* 152(6): 388–423.

Vince Lombardi quotes. 247 Sports. https://247sports.com/Coach/3614/Quotes/Individual-commitment-to-a-group-effort-that-is-what-makes-a-tea-35987286/

Walker, C. J. (2010). Experiencing flow: Is doing it together better than doing it alone? *The Journal of Positive Psychology* 5(1): 3–11.

Wyatt, C. (2021, May 3). What Phil Jackson's leadership teaches us about remote team-building. *Entrepreneur*. https://www.entrepreneur.com/leadership/what-phil-jacksons-leadership-teaches-us-about-remote/369620

Part II

Flow 2.0 Across Life Contexts

4

Flow 2.0

New Digital and the Hybrid World of Work

Mihaly wrote his books *Flow* (1990), *Good Work* (2001), and *Good Business* (2003) long before the COVID-19 global pandemic and our new digital and hybrid world of work. However, we argue in this chapter that many of his contributions to positive psychology and flow theory are even more important now when more than one-third of the working population in the US and Canada are remote or hybrid workers (Barrero et al. 2021; StatCan 2021). Harter (2023) argued that work engagement (and probably flow at work) is at its lowest level in a decade, and new strategies for enhancing optimal experience and functioning for workers, leaders, and organizations are sorely needed.

Workplace as the Setting for Finding Flow

The US Surgeon General (2022) recently published a national report on "Workplace Mental Health and Well-being," and discussed how the global pandemic has provided us an opportunity to rethink how we work. As Mihaly advocated for many years, the workplace is one of the most important settings for finding and fostering flow, connection, meaning, and well-being in people's lives. After all, most people spend the majority of their waking hours engaged in work or work-related activities (such as education and job preparation). The US Surgeon General highlights how important it is post-pandemic to design work

Flow 2.0: Optimal Experience in a Complex World. Honoring Mihaly Csikszentmihalyi's Legacy, First Edition. Stewart I. Donaldson and Matthew Dubin.
© 2025 John Wiley & Sons Ltd. Published 2025 by John Wiley & Sons Ltd.

environments (including digital, remote, and hybrid work) that support well-being, optimal experience, and positive functioning:

> *There are more than 160 million people who are a part of the US workforce today. Work is one of the most vital parts of life, powerfully shaping our health, wealth, and well-being. At its best, work provides us the ability to support ourselves and our loved ones, and can also provide us with a sense of meaning, opportunities for growth, and a community. When people thrive at work, they are more likely to feel physically and mentally healthy overall, and to contribute positively to their workplace. This creates both a responsibility and unique opportunity for leaders to create workplace environments that support the health and well-being of workers.*
>
> *(US Surgeon General 2022)*

Mihaly's foresight to create a field of positive psychology in 1998 has resulted in a timely and useful evidence base that can be used to promote health, well-being, optimal experience, and positive functioning in the evolving digital and hybrid work environment of 2024 and beyond. In the next section, the development and opportunities for this body of empirical research will be discussed.

Positive Psychology Goes to Work

Mihaly highlighted that decades of research demonstrated the importance and the challenges of the "negativity bias." In general, leaders, managers, and workers in the workplace tend to pay more attention to negative experiences than neutral or positive experiences at work. This bias likely developed early on in our evolution as an effective survival mechanism, but may have become less adaptive in the modern workplace. His vision was to inspire workplace researchers to move beyond the almost sole focus on what goes wrong, problems, deficits, and help people and organizations moved from a dysfunctional state into the "normal" range. He encouraged us to provide a more balanced perspective on well-being and positive functioning at work, and to aspire to understand both deficits and strengths, as part of the new science and practice of positive psychology.

Building on his ideas, Luthans (2002a) expanded on his vision and offered positive organizational behavior (POB), aiming for a more balanced approach to studying important topics in the workplace. He defined POB as "the study and application of positively oriented human resource strengths and psychological capacities that can be measured, developed, and effectively managed for performance in today's workplace" (Luthans 2002b, p. 59). POB focuses on identifying, measuring, and enhancing the strengths and psychological abilities of employees to improve their performance. Following Luthans, Cameron and others (2003) developed a similar concept called positive organizational scholarship (POS), which looks at the positive aspects of organizations that contribute to flourishing and well-being. POS was defined as the study of that which is positive, flourishing, and life giving in organizations.

Donaldson and Ko in their seminal article "Positive Organizational Psychology, Behavior, and Scholarship: A Review of the Emerging Literature and Evidence Base" took stock of the peer-reviewed empirical research that had resulted from studies in the first decade of positive psychology in the work context, POB, and POS. They introduced positive organizational psychology (POP) as a comprehensive term to encompass the extensive literature and empirical data base that had emerged to enhance the understanding of topics more aligned with strengths, to balance out the more extensive understanding of problems and deficits related to workplace experiences and behavior. POP was defined as "the scientific study of positive subjective experiences and traits in the workplace and positive organizations, and its application to improve the effectiveness and quality of life in organizations" (Donaldson and Ko 2010).

More than 14 years after its inception, POP has grown significantly. Mihaly's vision has been realized as it's now a well-established field studied in universities, with courses and programs dedicated to it. POP has led to many evidence-based practices and interventions designed to support the well-being and performance of employees, teams, and organizations, helping them to thrive and achieve their full potential.

Positive Psychology in the Workplace 2.0

The rapidly changing nature of work poses many challenges for leaders, managers, workplace researchers, and organizational development practitioners. The next wave of positive psychology studies in the workplace will inevitably be focused on how to enhance well-being and positive functioning in digital, remote, and hybrid workplaces facilitated by a wide range of new technologies. For example, Van Zyl et al. (2023) recently suggested POP 2.0 must embrace this technological revolution to remain relevant in the future. Some of the important trends they suggested to pay attention to include:

- "**Decentralization of work**: the rise of remote work and the gig economy has created challenges for traditional organizational structures and dynamics that POP has long investigated.
- "**Increases in data-driven approaches to assessment and development initiatives**: This growing emphasis on using big data to inform organizational decision-making, from hiring to retention and succession planning, has posed new challenges for POP. While data-driven approaches can provide valuable insights, they risk reducing complex human phenomena to mere numbers, which is antithetical to the human-centered approach promoted by positive psychology.
- "**Automation of human processes**: Technological advancements have become ubiquitous in organizations seeking to leverage these technologies as both competitive advantage and cost-saving mechanisms. This proliferation of accessible technology has led to innumerable tasks that were once done by humans now being done by automated systems. The effects on worker well-being are a growing concern as the implementation of automated systems – although linked to efficiency – creates disruption of other organizational systems, including workplace dynamics, organizational structure, and aspects of organizational culture.
- "**Artificial intelligence, social robots, and virtual workspaces**: The burgeoning science and application of AI, robots, and virtual work technologies have similarly upended traditional models of how workers interact, collaborate, and perform their tasks; the implications of which are barely beginning to be researched and understood."

The technologically enhanced digital, remote, and hybrid workplaces of the future will offer many new opportunities for workers, leaders, and organizations. Mihaly's vast contributions to developing a field of positive psychology that can be applied in dynamic and rapidly changing workplaces are notable. Below, we will shine a particularly bright light on his contributions to helping understand how to make work engaging and full of a wide range of optimal experiences.

Work Engagement and Flow

Many surveys report that workers on average tend to be highly disengaged post–COVID-19, and experience severe performance issues as a result (e.g., US Surgeon General 2022). Yan and Donaldson (2023) systematically reviewed the scientific literature on the related concepts of engagement and flow, and both were found to be commonly applied in various types of workplaces. However, flow interventions tended to be implemented especially often in sports, and sports oriented workplaces and organizations. The results of the evaluations of these flow interventions were largely positive, and the benefits of creating more flow and optimal experiences at work seemed valuable to workers, leaders, and organizations.

Mihaly elaborated on his profound thoughts about the importance of positive psychology and optional experiences at work in his best-selling book *Good Business: Leadership, Flow, and the Making of Meaning* (2003). He believed that work had become the center of contemporary life and had replaced religion and politics as the central forces. His writing illustrated how workers, managers, and business leaders can find flow in their work and create organizations characterized by fostering trust, personal growth, and optimal experiences for employees, and focused on serving the greater good while working on their own profit and sustainability. Some of Mihaly's important quotes reflecting his work on positive psychology and flow in the workplace include:

> *Attention is like energy in that without it no work can be done, and in doing work is dissipated. We create ourselves by how we use this energy. Memories, thoughts and feelings are all shaped by how use it. And it is an energy under control, to do with as we please; hence attention is our most important tool in the task of improving the quality of experience.*
>
> — *Csikszentmihalyi (1990)*

> *The best moments in our lives, are not the passive, receptive, relaxing times—although such experiences can also be enjoyable, if we have worked hard to attain them. The best moments usually occur when a person's body or mind is stretched to its limits in a voluntary effort to accomplish something difficult and worthwhile.*
>
> — *Csikszentmihalyi (1990)*

> *Optimal experience is thus something that we make happen. For a child, it could be placing with trembling fingers the last block on a tower she has built, higher than any she has built so far; for a swimmer, it could be trying to beat his own record; for a violinist, mastering an intricate musical passage. For each person there are thousands of opportunities, challenges to expand ourselves.*
>
> — *Csikszentmihalyi (1990)*

Leaders need to know what makes their followers tick:

> *On the job people feel skillful and challenged, and therefore feel more happy, strong, creative, and satisfied. In their free time people feel that there is generally not much to do and their skills are not being used, and therefore they tend to feel more sad, weak, dull, and dissatisfied. Yet they would like to work less and spend more time in leisure.*
>
> — *Csikszentmihalyi (1990)*

> *What does this contradictory pattern mean? There are several possible explanations, but one conclusion seems inevitable: when it comes to work, people do not heed the evidence of their senses. They disregard the quality of immediate experience, and base their motivation instead on the strongly rooted cultural stereotype of what work is supposed to be like. They think of it as an imposition, a constraint, an infringement of their freedom, and therefore something to be avoided as much as possible.*
>
> — *Csikszentmihalyi (1990)*

Sustaining Focus at Work in the Age of Distraction

This rise of digital technology has had a profound impact on people's ability to focus their attention. According to a study by the Microsoft Corporation (Borreli 2015), the human attention span has decreased to 8 seconds, which is 4 seconds less than the 12-second attention span found in the year 2000. While far more information is available to us, this accelerated technological age of constant information is not being matched by an increased capacity for humans to take in information. The nervous system has limits regarding how much information can be processed at any time, with Mihaly (1990) concluding that humans can process seven bits (i.e., different sounds, specific thoughts or emotions, visual stimuli) of information at any given time, which adds to a maximum of 126 bits of information per second, or 185 billion bits of information in a lifetime where every single aspect of one's life must take place, from thoughts, to emotions, to actions. With the prevalence of modern technology, individuals are constantly inundated with bits of information, from face-to-face interactions and environmental stimuli to the technological bits ranging from emails, text messages, and all that the internet has to offer. As Mihaly (1990) notes, these numbers regarding bits of information are suggestive, and it is a possibility that people constantly come up with effective strategies (e.g., "chunking") to deal with the increased intake of information. However, it stands to reason that individuals' attention spans have decreased in an adaptive attempt to keep up with the increase in attentional demands (i.e., information bits) that one is exposed to in daily life.

One of the supposed benefits of work today is how much information can be accessed, shared, and transferred instantaneously. However, an overload of information, if not properly managed, can be a massive impediment to achieving flow at work. In many cases, information can be synonymous with distraction. On a typical Zoom call, you can simultaneously be receiving information from the person talking, the other faces on the screen, your own face, your email inbox(es), web browser(s), texts/social media on your phone, and whatever else may be happening in your physical space (e.g., dog barking if working from home, colleagues walking by if in an office). How is complete immersion and concentration remotely possible with this modern work setup?

One of the more surprising findings from Mihaly's research was what he called "The Paradox of Work." While most individuals would prefer to spend their time in leisure and avoid work, they report having some of their most positive experiences at work while often reporting low moods during their leisure time (Csikszentmihalyi and LeFevre 1989). A potential explanation for this is that many jobs inherently possess flow's parameters and characteristics, such as the opportunities to use one's skills, the presence of challenge, immediate feedback, clear goals, and the potential for total concentration (Csikszentmihalyi 1990, 2003; Fullagar and Kelloway 2009, 2013). The more complex and intrinsically motivating a job is, the more likely flow becomes and the more likely an individual will want to further pursue their work (Csikszentmihalyi 1997; Csikszentmihalyi and LeFevre 1989; Crooke 2008; Harackiewicz et al. 1998).

While flow at work is similar to flow in any context, Bakker (2005) characterizes flow in the workplace as being a *short-term* peak experience where one is completely involved in what they are doing, accompanied by flow's other usual components such as time distortion and the merging of action and awareness. In his study of flow's antecedents at work, Bakker (2005) found that the job characteristics of autonomy, social support, and feedback predict flow's occurrence at work. Resources, both at the personal (i.e., self-efficacy) and organizational (i.e., social support, clear goals, innovation) level, have been found to increase flow's prevalence at work (Salanova et al. 2006; Fullagar and Kelloway 2013) and flow on the job has been found to decrease work exhaustion (Zito et al. 2015).

Other job characteristics suggested to increase flow at work include skill variety and the significance of the work task (Demerouti 2006; Donaldson and Ko 2010; Fullagar and Kelloway 2009). Specific job activities that have been found to predict flow include problem solving, planning, and evaluation (Nielsen and Cleal 2010).

A study that examined 10 working days of participants via diary found that day-specific flow experiences were found to mediate the relationship between affective commitment and a worker's day-specific well-being, as well as help employees more effectively deal with demands on self-control (Rivkin et al. 2016). Furthermore, flow at work has been found to be associated with employee creativity and to act as a mediator between authentic leadership and employee creativity (Zubair and Kamal 2015). For individuals who are high in conscientiousness, frequent flow experiences have been found to improve both in-role and extra-role performance (Demerouti 2006), and flow is associated with motivation, positive mood, and enjoyment in the context of work (Donaldson and Ko 2010; Fullagar and Kelloway 2009; Martin and Jackson 2008).

Theoretically, a lot of these characteristics are still very attainable on the job: We can still have clear goals, immediate feedback, a sense of autonomy, and challenge. However, the Dam of Distractions has become, far and away, the biggest consistent impediment to the flow stream at work. COVID-19 always forced millions of people who were used to working in an office to work from home, and many of these companies have permanent shifted their policies to stay fully remote or, even more common, a hybrid work arrangement. There is a raging debate about what arrangement is best for collaboration for performance, with many senior leaders strongly pushing for employees to come back to the office full-time. This debate undermines an essential truth for well-being, performance, and flow: There is no one-size-fits-all approach. Flow will look different for each person depending on a myriad of factors: Their natural personality traits, the team they inhabit in the organization, their job-level, location, and their previous personal/professional experiences.

Facilitating Flow at Work

In Dubin's (2018) dissertation, he interviewed knowledge workers to better understand the enablers and inhibitors of flow, as well as strategies to find flow amidst constant distraction. See Table 4.1 for a breakdown.

Based on this research and utilizing flow's general dimensions, there are several tactical shifts we can make to enable our own flow experiences at work:

1) *Identify our preferences and peak creative and productive times*. Some of us prefer the serenity of the early morning to do individual work, whereas some of us are night owls and feel a burst of energy when the sun goes down. Some of us prefer to think through an idea before discussing, and some of us prefer to work through our thoughts out loud. Gaining self-awareness about ourselves and where our energy comes from is a step towards structuring our lives in a more flow-conducive direction.
2) *Create mechanisms for self-feedback*. At work, it can often be difficult to know whether we're making the right type of progress or the wrong type of progress when working on a task. While consistent feedback from a manager is important, many of us don't get enough feedback, or don't have a manager at all. Therefore, whenever we create something at work that either makes us proud or receives positive feedback from a manager, client, or peer, we should "study" those victories in the same way a basketball team would review footage from a game to see what went well and what they can improve. Therefore, when working on something similar, moving forward, we have a reference point of what success looks like and begin to give ourselves feedback to know if we are on track and making meaningful progress.
3) *Stack like-minded tasks*. If we have a meeting from 1 to 1:30, then a break from 1:30 to 2, then another meeting from 2 to 2:30, then another break from 2:30 to 3, then a meeting again at 3 p.m., say

Table 4.1 Summary of flow enablers, inhibitors, and strategies from Dubin's (2018) dissertation.

1) *Factors Important for Enabling Flow*		2) *Factors Important for Inhibiting Flow*	
Headphones and noise levels	• Wearing headphones/ earbuds • Noise level distractions	**People interruptions**	• In-person interruptions • Technology interruptions
Having a clear direction	• Knowing what to do and where to go	**Urgent tasks/ priorities**	• Boss priorities • Tasks
Positive leadership	• Setting example • Providing autonomy • Providing challenge	**Suboptimal personal state**	• Psychological • Physical
Optimal personal state	• Physical • Pressure of deadline • Psychological	**Nature of projects**	• Lack of clarity • Lack of control
Impact of co-workers	• Contagious flow • Collaborating with others		
3) *Strategies to Facilitate Flow at Work*			
Organizing time and tasks	• To-do list • Timing tasks • Block out calendar for "flow" time Prioritizing tasks		
Managing technology use	• Put phone away • Managing notifications • Focus apps • Printing Delete apps		
Mental health and wellness	• Take a break • Food/beverage • Exercise • Meditation • Yoga • Sleep • Balance		

Table 4.1 (Continued)

Change location	• Work away from office Separate room in office
Leadership	• Respect • Feedback • Autonomy
Wearing headphones/ Listening to music	• Headphones/music at work
Being prepared and having a direction	• Satisfaction of being productive • Meetings • Establishing clear direction

Source: With permission of Dubin 2018.

goodbye to any sense of flow or accomplishment in that block of time. It would be far more flow conducive to have those three meetings be back-to-back, then give ourselves 90 minutes of uninterrupted time afterwards to fully dive into another activity. When we shift between tasks that frequently, we do not give ourselves enough time to fully dive into something meaningful, and it also takes a mental toll to context switch so frequently. A choppy day will feel busy but often lack energy or a sense of accomplishment.

4) *Give your presence and focus to receive it back.* Our personal favorite finding from Dubin's (2018) dissertation is that flow is contagious – our energy and engagement affect the energy and engagement of those we interact with, and vice versa. It's important to tend to each interaction with care and attention. If we bring that to our interactions, we will be more likely to receive it from the other person, and they are more likely to pay it forward in their future interactions that day.
5) *Have your pre-flow rituals.* To ensure that our minds and bodies are set up to have a flow experience, we must also have rituals in place that enable us to fully dive into something afterward. Oftentimes people wake up in the morning and have a routine that gets the day started right – whether it's walking their dog, spending time with their family, having a leisurely breakfast while reading a newspaper, or exercising. Setting aside time for these rituals prepares us to have a successful workday, more mentally prepared to manage the various challenges and stresses that make up a job.

Conclusion

While these steps are the place to start, there is a deeper layer to finding sustained flow at work. Removing distractions and making tactical shifts in our day's structure paves the roads clear for flow, but we still need to figure out how to actually drive down that path. This starts with our mental health. Caring for our minds and bodies, through nutrition, exercise, sleep, and breaks ensures we have a working engine. If our mind and body aren't right, it is very difficult for flow to ensue no matter how many of its conditions are present. So, once the roads are clear and our engine is working, then we can begin to craft our work experience in a more holistic way to sustain flow.

Some of this is within our control, but leaders also play an essential role in cultivating the conditions of flow for their people. As an individual, for example, we can set clear microgoals in our work, but the overall macrogoals of knowing what we're working toward and how our work is contributing to the bigger picture is often decided and communicated by our leaders. Having a sense of autonomy in our work, a key factor for flow on the job, is also largely not within the personal control of employees but established by their managers.

Leaders also set the tone of how much their people feel like they can speak up at work without repercussion, where they can ask questions and bring new ideas to the table freely, which helps facilitate group flow. With the finding that flow is contagious, every single person within a company has a role to play in the overall flow-conduciveness of the organization. While we should make the necessary tweaks to enhance our own flow state, flow in organizations is a collective process, with each person, whether a leader or individual contributor playing an indispensable role in the daily experience of those they work with.

Most people spend the majority of their waking hours working or involved in work-related activities (e.g., education or training for work and careers). Mihaly has provided us with many insights about how to make the quality of our waking hours at work as fulfilling and productive as possible. He has encouraged us all to seek good work (Csikszentmihalyi and LeFevre 1989), practice good business (Csikszentmihalyi 2003), and to craft our work and careers in a way that produces flow and optimal experiences. Of course, it is up to us now to apply his ideas in our own work and careers in the complex digital workplaces we are likely to face, and to improve others' individual and collective well-being and positive functioning in the work environments of today and tomorrow (see US Surgeon General 2022).

References

Aksoy, C. G., Barrero, J. M., Bloom, N., Davis, S. J., Dolls, M., and Zarate, P. 2022). Working from home around the world. *CESifo Forum* 23(6): 38–41. https://doi.org/10.2139/ssrn.4219442

Bakker, A. B. (2005). Flow among music teachers and their students: The crossover of peak experiences. *Journal of Vocational Behavior* 66: 26–44.

Barrero, J. M., Bloom, N., and Davis, S. J. (2021). *Why working from home will stick* (No. 28731). http://www.nber.org/papers/w28731

Beňo, M. (2021). The advantages and disadvantages of e-working: An examination using an aldine analysis. *Emerging Science Journal* 5(Special issue): 11–20. https://doi.org/10.28991/esj-2021-SPER-02

Borreli, L. (2015, May 14). *Human attention span shortens to 8 seconds due to digital technology: 3 ways to stay focused.* Retrieved from http://www.medicaldaily.com/human-attention-span-shortens-8-seconds-due-digital-technology-3-ways-stay-focused-333474

Cameron, K. S., Dutton, J. E., and Quinn, R. E. (2003). *Positive Organizational Scholarship: Foundations for a New Discipline.* San Francisco, CA: Berrett-Koehler.

Crooke, M. W. (2008). *A Mandala for Organizations in the 21st Century.* Doctoral dissertation. Claremont Graduate University, Claremont, CA.

Csikszentmihalyi, M. (1990). *Flow: The Psychology of Optimal Experience.* New York: HarperCollins.

Csikszentmihalyi, M. (1997). *Finding Flow: The Psychology of Engagement with Everyday Life.* New York: HarperCollins.

Csikszentmihalyi, M. (2003). *Good Business: Leadership, Flow, and the Making of Meaning.* New York: Viking.

Csikszentmihalyi, M. and LeFevre, J. (1989). Optimal experience in work and leisure. *Journal of Personality and Social Psychology* 56: 815–822.

Demerouti, E. (2006). Job characteristics, flow, and performance: The moderating role of conscientiousness. *Journal of Occupational Health Psychology* 11(3): 266–208.

Donaldson, S. I. and Ko, I. (2010). Positive organizational psychology, behavior, and scholarship: A review of the emerging literature and evidence base. *Journal of Positive Psychology* 5(3): 177–191.

Dubin, M. (2018). Experiencing flow at work as a digital native in an accelerated knowledge economy (doctoral dissertation). Claremont Graduate University, Claremont, CA.

Fullagar, C. and Kelloway, E. K. (2009). Flow at work: An experience sampling approach. *Journal of Occupational and Organizational Psychology* 82: 595–615.

Fullagar, C. and Kelloway, E. K. (2013). Work-related flow. In A. Bakker, and K. Daniels (eds.), *A Day in the Life of a Happy Worker* (pp. 41–57). London: Psychology Press.

Galanti, T., Guidetti, G., Mazzei, E., Zappalà, S., and Toscano, F. (2021). Work from home during the COVID-19 outbreak: The impact on employees' remote work productivity, engagement, and stress. *Journal of Occupational and Environmental Medicine* 63(7): E426–E432. https://doi.org/10.1097/JOM.0000000000002236

Harackiewicz, J. M., Barron, K.E., and Elliot, A.J. (1998). Rethinking achievement goals: When are they adaptive for college students and why? *Educational Psychologist* 33(1): 1–21.

Harter, J. (2023). US employee engagement needs a rebound in 2023. https://www.gallup.com/workplace/468233/employee-engagement-needs-rebound-2023.aspx

Luthans, F. (2002a). The need for and meaning of positive organizational behavior. *Journal of Organizational Behavior: The International Journal of Industrial, Occupational and Organizational Psychology and Behavior* 23(6): 695–706.

Luthans, F. (2002b). Positive organizational behavior: Developing and managing psychological strengths. *Academy of Management Perspectives* 16(1): 57–72.

Martin, A. J. and Jackson, S. A. (2008). Brief approaches to assessing task absorption and enhanced subjective experience: Examining 'short' and 'core' flow in diverse performance domains. *Motivation and Emotion* 32: 141–157.

Nielsen, K. and Cleal, B. (2010). Predicting flow at work: Investigating the activities and job characteristics that predict flow states at work. *Journal of Occupational Health Psychology* 15(2): 180–190.

Rivkin, W., Diestel, S., and Schmidt, K. H. (2016). Which daily experiences can foster well-being at work? A diary study on the interplay between flow experiences, affective commitment, and self-control demands. *Journal of Occupational Health Psychology* 23(1). https://doi.org/10.1037/ocp0000039

Salanova, M., Bakker, A. B. and Llorens, S. (2006). Flow at work: Evidence for an upward spiral of personal and organizational resources. *Journal of Happiness Studies* 7: 1–22.

StatCan. (2021). Working from home during the COVID-19 pandemic, April 2020 to June 2021. https://www150.statcan.gc.ca/n1/pub/36-28-0001/2022008/article/00001-eng.htm

US Surgeon General (2022). The US Surgeon General's framework for workplace mental health and well-being. https://www.hhs.gov/surgeongeneral/priorities/workplace-well-being/index.html

Van Zyl, L., Gaffaney, J., Van der Vaart, L., Dik, B., and Donaldson, S. I. (2023). The critiques and criticisms of positive psychology: A systematic review. *Journal of Positive Psychology.*

Yan, Q. and Donaldson, S. I. (2023). What are the differences between flow and work engagement? A systematic review of positive intervention research. *The Journal of Positive Psychology* 18(3): 449–459. https://doi.org/10.1080/17439760.2022.2036798

Zito, M., Cortese, C. G., and Colombo, L. (2015). Nurses' exhaustion: The role of flow at work between job demands and job resources. *Journal of Nursing Management* 24(1): 12–22.

Zubair, A. and Kamal, A. (2015). Authentic leadership and creativity: Mediating role of work-related flow and psychological capital. *Journal of Behavioural Sciences* 25(1): 150–171.

5

Finding Flow in Sports and Leisure Pursuits

The motivation orientation toward work will always begin extrinsically – our paychecks are non-negotiable. That will always add a layer of complexity towards finding flow at work, since most of us *have* to work whether we are able to find intrinsically motivating factors or not. With our leisure time, however, motivation for pursuing any particular activity is more naturally intrinsic – the activities we pursue are generally because we want to, not because we have to. However, the activities we naturally choose to do are often not the activities that would enable flow. If we've had a long, exhausting day at work or raising young children, we may choose to spend our leisure time curled up on the couch with a cozy blanket, scrolling our phones endlessly until we fall asleep. When many of these types of days compound, it creates a sense of "meh" in our daily experience that goes unaddressed because there's nothing wrong, per se, but not much is going totally right either. On December 3, 2021, after almost two years of the COVID-19 pandemic, Organizational Psychologist Adam Grant wrote an article in the *New York Times* that articulated the emotion so many of us were feeling at that time, and in the time since: "languishing." The "neglected middle child of mental health… It wasn't burnout – we still had energy. It wasn't depression – we didn't feel hopeless. We just felt somewhat joyless and aimless." Grant describes languishing as "a sense of stagnation and emptiness. It feels as if you're muddling through your days, looking at your life through a foggy "windshield." Later in the article, Grant explains that flow may be the antidote to languishing, and that

Flow 2.0: Optimal Experience in a Complex World. Honoring Mihaly Csikszentmihalyi's Legacy, First Edition. Stewart I. Donaldson and Matthew Dubin.
© 2025 John Wiley & Sons Ltd. Published 2025 by John Wiley & Sons Ltd.

experiencing flow during the early days of the pandemic was the best predictor of well-being. While we cannot necessarily control all elements of our work experience to find flow as much as we'd optimally choose, we should be able to pursue leisure activities that provide flow at a higher rate, which would provide more sharpness and clarity to our daily experience, and steer clear of languishing. This chapter will explore flow within the domains of leisure and sports, with the goal of better understanding how flow can be achieved in these domains no matter where our interests may lie.

Flow and Leisure

The list of leisure activities that can provide flow for us is boundless. While there isn't necessarily a set, agreed upon definition of leisure, one analysis (Primeau 1996, as cited in Perkins and Nakamura 2012) explicated that there are three ways we can define these types of activities:

1) The residual time outside of work, or other forms of productive or maintenance activities
2) The set of activities that people within a particular culture identify as a leisure pursuit
3) A positive experience that is chosen freely and is intrinsically rewarding

Therefore, if it is an activity outside of work, that we choose to do in our free time that provides us joy, it can be considered a leisure pursuit. When I (Dubin) lead workshops on flow for organizations, I usually ask participants to name an activity where they find flow outside of work. The most common responses are cooking/baking, reading, playing an instrument, solving a puzzle, gaming, writing, gardening, a conversation with those of similar interests, cleaning/organizing (always surprises me), and watching an engrossing TV series. No matter what activity someone offers, I'm always thrilled when someone can name at least one – something in their daily routine that provides that active, immersive state of control, clarity, and feedback. According to the early days of leisure theory, the social psychological constructs of *perceived freedom* and *intrinsic motivation* are essential to for the prevalence and quality of leisure activities (Iso-Ahola 1979; Mannell 1984; Neulinger 1974, 1981; Tinsley and Tinsley 1986). David Melnikoff, an assistant professor of organizational behavior at the Stanford Graduate School of Business, indicates that there's no clear time frame for entering flow, but it depends on the complexity of the task and your familiarity with it (as cited in Dunn 2024).

Going with the Flow

Here are five questions to ask yourself when pursuing flow-conducive leisure activities:

1) Are You Trying to Engage Your Body or Your Mind?
Some people's preferred flow activities are physical (playing a sport, running, lifting weights), which primarily engages our bodies. Other flow activities are more mental (reading a book, working on a puzzle, writing). As Mihaly (1990) says:

> *The good things in life do not come only through the sense. Some of the most exhilarating experiences we undergo are generated inside the mind, triggered by information that challenges our ability to think, rather than from the use of sensory skills…Just as there are flow activities corresponding to every physical potential of the body, every mental operation is able to provide its own particular form of enjoyment.*
>
> *(Csikszentmihalyi 1990, p. 117)*

Some flow activities combine both mental and physical engagement, such as yoga or playing certain musical instruments. Each individual generally has a natural proclivity to each type of activity, where they find one far more intrinsically motivating than the other. Some are just naturally drawn to sports or exercising and the feeling it provides during and after, while others only pursue these activities extrinsically to stay healthy and in shape. Even within the domain of physical activity, some find certain individual activities to be boring (e.g., running) but others to be conducive of flow (e.g., taking a spin class). Ultimately, all that matters is that you know what's right for you, and why. Some people love the in-person energy of a packed spin class, whereas others find the lack of personal space overwhelming and anxiety-inducing, preferring a solitary run. Some prefer to play off teammates in a team sport (basketball or soccer), and some prefer to be completely self-reliant and in complete control of the situation (tennis or golf). What's important is that we are aware of what we are drawn to at our core – not what others think we should do, or that pleases someone else. There is enough in life that we must do for extrinsic reasons that we should not have that mindset interfere with our leisure choices. However, we sometimes become so accustomed to accommodating others that we lose sight of what we find intrinsically motivating, and therefore spend our leisure time in misalignment with our personal preferences and values.

2) How Much Time Can You Devote?

The measure of progress for leisure activities varies. Some use the clock (watching the time tick down on a 30-minute spin class) to indicate progress, whereas others use a checklist, for example (moving through baking instructions or a LEGO assembly manual). When you are pressed for time, it wouldn't make sense to pursue a flow activity where you could get lost in it for hours, like diving into an engrossing book only to feel like you were out of time when you were just getting started. However, you may have time to complete a crossword puzzle within your 25-minute window. Ensuring that you embark on an activity where you can make meaningful progress given the time you have will be far more flow conducive than feeling you barely scratched the surface. On the other hand, if you give yourself too much time to complete a task, Parkinson's law will often come into effect — the concept that work expands to fill the time allotted to complete it. Therefore, if you give yourself an hour to complete a crossword puzzle that you could complete in 25 minutes, you will naturally move at a slower pace and be more prone to distraction to fill the hour you gave yourself to complete the task.

3) What Makes Sense for the Rhythm of Your Body, Mind, and Life Circumstances?

Those who regularly exercise tend to have a strong preference for working out in the morning (before work, childcare, class, etc.) or closer to the end of the day. This natural proclivity to knowing when your body will best react to exercise is essential to setting yourself up for a flow conducive experience. The same is true for mentally focused activities. Some people would prefer to engage their minds first thing in the morning and are too tired after work to complete a complex mental task outside of their jobs. Or perhaps, someone who watches children for the majority of the day would prefer to pursue a flow activity that would provide peace and quiet, such as reading, when they are able to have a moment of leisure. Meanwhile, the individual who works at a quiet desk all day would far prefer to meet others for dinner and conversation. Our minds and bodies must be prepared to enter flow successfully, which will depend on physical, mental, and personality preferences, as well as our life circumstances. Introverts will usually have a proclivity for more solitary flow activities, but not always, especially if their work provides a lot of solitude already (e.g., an individual who works mainly from home on their own). Extroverts will generally prefer more collective flow activities, but again, not always, depending on their life circumstances.

4) What Is Intrinsically Motivating?
As described in Chapter 2, intrinsic motivation is one of the core characteristics of flow: When you pursue something for the sake of it. The activity is inherently joyful, and you do not need any extrinsic validation – whether it be money, status, or recognition – to continue pursuing the activity. In order to know what is intrinsically motivating for you, *New York Times* columnist Jancee Dunn suggests we go flow hunting:

> *Write down five of the most deeply immersive moments you had last year. Where were you and what were you doing? Do those moments have anything in common? Maybe they all took place outdoors or involved other people. This list can help you figure out what gets you in the flow. Your past interests and hobbies can also provide clues. What did you love to do when you were younger? If you could go back to school for a year, what would you study?*

If playing video games was flow conducive for you as a teenager, chances are you will still find joy and immersion through similar forms of gaming today – but maybe you don't have time or think you have "matured" past that point in your life. Games of any kind (video/mobile games, board/puzzle games, etc.) inherently contain many of the characteristics that will consistently induce flow: a clear goal, balancing your skills with an attainable challenge, and deep concentration. The types of games you find conducive of flow may change, depending on your interests, but the relationship between games and immersive enjoyment is evergreen.

5) How Am I Feeling in the Present Moment?
Dan Gilbert, a Harvard Professor and author of the brilliant book, *Stumbling on Happiness*, says, "At every stage of our lives, we make decisions that will profoundly influence the lives of the people we're going to become. Then when we become those people, we're not always thrilled with the decisions we made." While Gilbert's point mainly pertains to decisions that will impact us years from now, they still apply at a more micro level. The cognitive decisions we make for ourselves may not match our emotional capacity to follow through on these plans when the time comes. For example, I may make dinner plans after work because I was feeling social and energized in the moment I made those plans, but I may not want to follow through on them when the time comes if I've had a work day full of stressful meetings. Of course, it would be rude to cancel on someone else just because we no longer felt like being social, but for our individual hobbies it is important to listen to our in-the-moment feelings. If I've been sitting all day at work, I may be itching for a physically active flow activity, whereas if I've been on my feet all day, I may prefer to sit and read a book or play video games. While it is important to stretch ourselves when we can even if we don't necessarily feel up for it (people never regret working out even if they felt tired beforehand), our bodies and minds can only be stretched so far, so it's important to consider how much stretching has already been done that day. The best we are capable of will differ by the day, so choosing a flow activity that we can realistically engage with given how we are feeling physically, emotionally, cognitively, and psychologically will enable greater success and fulfillment.

Flow, TV, and Video Games

Dunn calls these types of flow activities "low stakes flow states." One of the most popular flow activities of this nature is watching TV shows – which has undergone a drastic shift in the last three decades since Mihaly's book. At that time, Mihaly's studies indicated that television watching was not a particularly enjoyable activity for participants, but they would still prefer to watch TV over work, even though work provided more engagement and enjoyment. He called this the "paradox of work." For primetime television in 1991–1992, four of the top five shows in terms of weekly viewers were sitcoms (*Roseanne, Murphy Brown, Cheers,* and *Home Improvement*, as cited in Brooks and Marsh 2007). Sitcoms are traditionally very "easy" to watch, designed for laughs and allowing viewers to shut off their brains. After that, the "prestige" TV era took place with shows like *The Sopranos, The Wire, Breaking Bad,* and *Mad Men,* more designed to challenge viewers with complex characters and story arcs. Other shows, such as *Lost* and *Game of Thrones*, also spurred obsessive internet engagement, with theories and deep dives about what would happen next, providing its own source of flow in between episodes. Therefore, the energy, concentration, and skill it took to engage with these shows increased substantially compared to the "easier" watches of sitcoms most common in the 1970s to 1990s.

With the advent of Netflix and the streaming era, where full seasons of TV would be released at once and we could now binge entire series, watching a 10-episode season of television in the span of a weekend became commonplace. Shows became more designed to "hook" their viewers and to be more binge-worthy, prompting us to compulsively let the next episode play to find out what happens next. The next episode would provide the "feedback" we desperately craved of having certain questions answered, but of course, new plot points would arise that would then demand their own set of answers, algorithmically designed to keep us immersed until the season ended. TV today can genuinely be a flow experience, as long as individuals put certain parameters in place. For example, watching five 1-hour episodes in a row will most likely result in "overflow," leading to fatigue with the content and general exhaustion from sitting in front of a screen for so many hours.

Also, a more recent phenomenon dubbed "ambient TV," discussed by Cultural Commentator Kyle Chayka in *The New Yorker* (2020), has become part of the culture, where a show serves a similar purpose as background music while we do something else, like scroll on our phones or check our email. Chayka describes the show "Emily in Paris" as an example of this:

> *The purpose of* Emily in Paris *is to provide sympathetic background for staring at your phone, refreshing your own feeds—on which you'll find* Emily in Paris *memes, including a whole genre of TikTok remakes. It's OK to look at your phone all the time, the show seems to say, because Emily does it, too. The episodic plots are too thin to ever be confusing; when you glance back up at the television,*

> *chances are that you'll find tracking shots of the Seine or cobblestoned alleyways, lovely but meaningless...Eventually, sensing that you've played two episodes straight without pausing or skipping, Netflix will ask if you're still really watching. Shamed, I clicked the Yes button, and Emily continued being in Paris.*

These kinds of shows are designed to only be as interesting as we need them to be, lending itself to the type of multi-screen distraction that would prevent flow from taking place. These types of shows seem keenly aware of our phone addictions, asking us to use them as a supplement to scrolling instead of a replacement. So, while TV watching *can* serve as a flow experience in ways that weren't possible in the second half of the twentieth century, it requires an intentionality over the content we choose and the concentration we devote to it, or it can become a vehicle for that sense of "blah" or languishing that is all too common.

While watching TV is a more passive activity, playing video games is a more active endeavor that is ripe for flow. Games are often designed with the purpose of immersing the player into the gaming experience, with clear goals, immediate feedback, and balancing the challenge with a player's developing skills, with a number of studies investigating the prevalence of flow within this medium (Chen 2007; Cowley et al. 2008; Jin 2012). Cowley (2012) identified four categories of game experiences that are inherent or related to flow:

1) *Effectance.* A feeling of empowerment that a player experiences when they can directly see the impact of their actions. This is closely tied to receiving "immediate feedback" throughout the game and the challenge of the game consistently matching our level of skill.
2) *Identification.* This occurs when we identify with the character in a game rather than ourselves. In an American football video game, for example, we take on the identity of the quarterback, a key component of the immersive nature of the experience.
3) *Transportation.* During a gaming experience, we are mentally transported to another world, allowing us to completely concentrate on the stimuli within the game and lose our sense of self-consciousness.
4) *Mental workload.* Games present a whole new set of cognitive stimuli that exists fully separate from the physical world, resulting in a substantial cognitive load for players that enables full concentration. Cowley states that for a game to enable flow, it must have "clear

unambiguous goals. Missions, plot, levels, quests, and explicit structures allow evaluating success of a gaming session. This relates to the ability of the human brain to only process a limited amount of information at a given time."

TV shows and video games both present opportunities for us to engage in a story or task that exists outside of the physical world and lend themselves to flow rather easily. Both mediums have also evolved at a rapid pace in the last three decades in the quest to maximize their immersive elements, which will only compound over the next three decades as gaming in the realm of virtual and augmented reality becomes more prevalent. While of course the internet has also become a source of flow in the context of leisure, this will be more deeply explored in Chapter 6.

Flow and Sports

"The human body is capable of hundreds of separate functions – seeing, hearing, touching, running, swimming, throwing, catching, climbing up mountains, and climbing down caves, to name only a few – and to each of these there correspond flow experiences" (Csikszentmihalyi 1990, p. 95). There are few areas of life that are more flow conducive than when we combine the functions of the body with the structure and competition of sport. Researchers have also linked flow among athletes with higher levels of performance, confidence, and the feeling of actions being "easy" or "automatic" (Harris et al. 2017; Jackson and Roberts 1992; Keller and Landhäußer 2012; Nakamura and Csikszentmihalyi 2002; Nicholls et al. 2015). When Golden State Warriors legend Steph Curry catches a ball from beyond the arc and looks at the rim, his goal is crystal clear: "I'm going to make this shot." In that particular moment, nothing else matters (Figure 5.1). Sometimes, he's so confident in achieving this goal that he starts running back to the other side of the court before the ball has even dropped through the hoop. He describes those moments as such: "It's the one time that everything kind of goes on autopilot. And there's just synergy with everything that you're trying to do. Even your intentions are then validated by the atmosphere around you. Where it seems like everything else is going right at the same time, you kind of get lost in that moment" (Caldwell 2023).

The flow state has been described by some of the greatest basketball players of all time. The late Lakers legend Kobe Bryant describes this zone similarly: "When you get in that zone, it's just supreme

Figure 5.1 Stephen Curry, Golden State Warriors, "shooting a three."
Source: Ezra Shaw/Getty Images.

confidence... Things just slow down. You really do not focus on what's going on. You have to really try to stay in the present and not let anything break that rhythm" (Vaughn et al. 2017). In 2024, after Lakers star LeBron James led a 21-point fourth-quarter comeback for his team, he described the feeling of being in flow: "I was just in the zone. I know we've kind of heard what it feels like to be in the zone in our sport, and it's just a feeling where you feel like everything you put up is going in...You wish you could stay in it forever, but obviously it checks out as the game ends. But during it you don't feel anything, it's just like a superpower I feel" (Linn 2024).

There is perhaps no ground that is more fertile for experiencing flow than sports, ranging from amateur to professional, as an individual or as part of a team. When one's body and mind are completely in sync, with crystal-clear micro and macro goals, achieving immediate feedback every step of the way, flow naturally ensues. It is through sport that the most colloquial term for flow, being "in the zone," came about. In fact, witnessing elite athletes in flow can be so captivating that even watching them can be a passive flow experience.

When Kansas City Chiefs quarterback Patrick Mahomes engineered a thrilling come-from-behind victory against the Buffalo Bills in the 2022 playoffs, he was wearing a Whoop heart monitor that tracked his heart rate throughout the game. His performance coach, Bobby Stroupe, posted a fascinating screenshot of his heart rate tracking after the game (Figure 5.2).

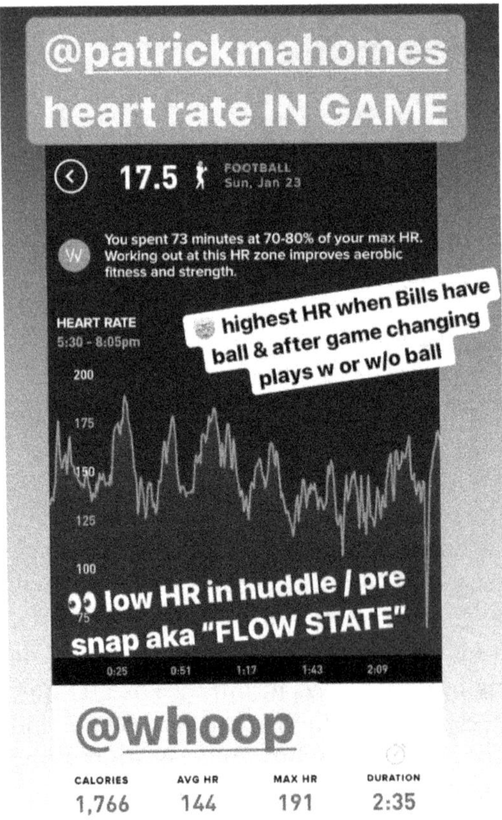

Figure 5.2 Bobby Stroupe, performance coach for Mahomes, posted a screenshot for the quarterback's heart rate during a 2022 playoff game: "Highest HR when Bills have the ball and after game changing plays w or w/o ball," and "low HR in huddle / pre snap aka 'FLOW STATE'."

In other words, his heart rate was far higher when the opposing team had the ball, and dropped significantly when he was leading huddles when his team had the ball. Wait, what?! From everything we know about physical activity, it would make sense to assume that the more effort he exerted, the higher his heart rate would spike. However, this finding indicates that when he felt in control of the situation, with his team having the ball and leading them through a pre-snap huddle, his body found a sense of serenity that dropped his heart rate. When in flow, it feels like a meditative calmness takes over our experience, as evidenced by Mahomes's heart rate in an extremely high-pressure situation.

Gold medalist swimmer Katie Ledecky (Figure 5.3) described this sense of calm upon breaking a World Record: "I felt so relaxed. It just felt very easy, and that's why it surprised me that I had broken my world record" (Vaughn et al. 2017).

While individuals like Mahomes, Curry, and Ledecky have crystal-clear in-the-moment goals (make the shot, complete the pass), teams also have crystal-clear objectives that keep them focused on a common goal (win the game, make the playoffs, win the championship). Sports offer a set of objective goals to strive for that is rarely found in other domains that consume our time – what is the equivalent of "winning a

Figure 5.3 Gold medal swimmer Katie Ledecky set a world record for the 1500 meter freestyle in at the World Cup in Toronto on October 29, 2022. *Source:* FRANCOIS-XAVIER MARIT/AFP/Getty Images.

championship" for the marketing department of a large corporation? The common goals a team shares keep everyone moving in the same direction, with the best teams never wavering in ensuring that every action they take is in service of the group's goal.

In sports, a very similar set of dimensions that were described in Chapter 2 apply to achieving flow in sports, as outlined by the preeminent flow-in-sports researcher, Susan Jackson (Jackson and Csikszentmihalyi 1999, p. 16), along with selected quotes from elite athletes and coaches describing their experience in that dimension:

1) *Challenge-skills balance.* "I guess it was the extreme challenge, but we didn't approach is as a major hurdle." (World Cup rugby finalist before the team's final game, p. 17)
2) *Action-awareness merging.* "It doesn't seem like you're sitting on a bike. You feel altogether like it's just one piece of machinery working together...like you're part of this machine that you were born with, and it's how you move." (anonymous elite Cyclist Jackson calls "Simon," p. 19)
3) *Clear goals.* "My short-term goals are obtainable on a daily or monthly basis. I like to make my short-term goals something that makes me feel better and sets me up to better prepare for the long-term goals." (Olympic Swimmer Jessica Hardy, as cited in Watkins Ross 2021)
4) *Unambiguous feedback.* "The purpose is to help, to prevent, to correct, to improve, rather than to punish. Criticism is not meant to punish, but rather to correct something that is preventing better results. The only goal is improvement." (Legendary UCLA Men's Basketball Coach John Wooden, retrieved from AZQuotes)
5) *Concentration on the task at hand.* "I was totally absorbed, 110 percent; that was all that mattered in the whole existence. It just amazed me how I could maintain such high concentration for three hours. I'm used to having my mind wander, especially under pressure." (Simon as cited in Jackson and Csikszentmihalyi 1999, p. 9)
6) *Sense of control.* "I never played perfect tennis in my career, but I did play matches where I felt in control and never left third gear." (Tennis Legend Andre Agassi 2020)
7) *Loss of self-consciousness.* "You have to lose yourself in the team and you have to lose yourself in the game." (Kentucky Head Men's Basketball Coach John Calipari, as cited in Morrison 2022)

8) *Transformation of time.* "When you work out or you're doing anything active, it's more fun as a group. You may lose track of the time, and the next thing you know, you're working out for two hours because you're having fun." (LeBron James, as cited in Nunley 2024)
9) *Autotelic experience.* "You are never really playing an opponent. You are playing yourself, your own highest standards, and when you reach your limits, that is real joy." (Tennis Legend Arthur Ashe, as cited in Stampone 2019)

Jackson and Csikszentmihalyi (1999, p. 12) also laid out the most common words and phrases that elite athletes used in their interviews to describe the flow experience (Table 5.1).

The barriers that exist to flow in other domains (digital technology distraction, ambiguous objectives, insecurity/self-consciousness, extrinsic motivation) do not run as rampantly in sports, thus helping to facilitate flow's more consistent occurrence. I (Dubin) play in an adult recreational men's basketball league (I'm a mediocre player at best), and the one-hour game every week is one of the few guaranteed sources of flow that I can count on amidst the clutter of daily life. Time flies by,

Table 5.1 Common words and phrases elite athletes use in their interviews.

In the bubble	Going really well
Complete satisfaction	Nothing else matters
Focused	Weightlessness
In the zone	In the groove
Total involvement	Optimal pace
Peaceful	Flowing
On auto	Tuned in
Everything clicks	In control
Switched on	Strong
Concentration	Total composure and confidence
Going fast and doing it easily	Floating
Ideal	Super alive
Unbeatable	Total control

Source: Jackson and Csikszentmihalyi (1999) / Human Kinetics.

and all of my professional and personal worries and anxieties melt away. The second the game ends, I check the time on my phone, and it's over. My mind immediately starts racing with the schedule for the next day, whether our baby will sleep through the night, and any other worries of the day. However, I feel more equipped to handle these items coming off the clarity of a flow experience, that unique feeling of transcending the daily grind even if it's just for an hour.

Dr. Susan Jackson and Mihaly wrote *Flow in Sports: The Keys to Optimal Experience and Performance* to focus entirely on the relationship between athletes and their ability to tap into flow more consistently. They describe the experience of participating in sports as such:

> *...now, most people are attracted to sport for more practical reasons: they hope to keep their weight or blood pressure down, want to excel over the competition, or dream of making a great deal of money in the professional leagues. But whatever other reasons motivate the athlete, the crux of sport is the* quality of experience *it provides. Contrary to what happens in most of life, sport can offer a state of being that is so rewarding one does for no other reason than to be a part of it.*
>
> *(Jackson and Csikszentmihalyi 1999)*

Conclusion

This chapter delved into two subjects that, for most of us, are pursued for largely intrinsic reasons: leisure and sports. As a result, they have been ripe domains for the study of flow and will continue to maintain an essential role in our daily experience and capacity to find flow in daily activities. Ralph Waldo Emerson has a brilliant take on leisure: "Guard well your spare moments. They are like uncut diamonds. Discard them and their value will never be known. Improve them and they will become the brightest gems in a useful life" (as cited in Hurtado 2023).

As so many of our lives seem to be getting busier, spending our leisure time exerting as little effort as possible, like sitting on the couch and scrolling social media, often feels like the most attractive option. However, the more intentional we are about selecting flow activities during our leisure time, the more we will actually feel energized and sharp, and more prepared to take on the next day. It's similar to how many of us feel before we exercise: We're often tired and don't feel like it, but we know if we do it, we absolutely won't regret it. Like exercise, once we start consistently pursuing flow activities in our leisure time, it becomes a habit that is baked into our daily routine.

Often, we will choose leisure activities that differ from how we spent our time at work: If we were with colleagues all day, for example, we may choose a leisure activity that doesn't require talking or socializing, but if we worked from home on our own, we may prefer to spend time with friends after work. Given your preferences and circumstances, choose what makes sense for you, for it is often the only time in the day that is truly your own.

References

AZ Quotes. John Wooden quotes about purpose. https://www.azquotes.com/author/15923-John_Wooden/tag/purpose

Agassi, A. (2020, July 10). *Andre Agassi...remembering 1992 wimbledon.* ATP Tour. https://www.atptour.com/en/news/agassi-1992-wimbledon-atp-heritage

Brooks, T. and Marsh, E. (2007). *The Complete Directory to Prime Time Network and Cable TVShows 1946–Present* (9th ed.). Ballantine Books.

Caldwell, H. (2023, March 1). *How do top athletes get in into the zone? By getting uncomfortable.* TED. https://ideas.ted.com/how-do-top-athletes-get-into-the-zone-by-getting-uncomfortable/

Chayka, K. (2020, November 16). "Emily in Paris" and the rise of ambient TV. *The NewYorker.* https://www.newyorker.com/culture/cultural-comment/emily-in-paris-and-the-rise-of-ambient-tv

Chen, J. (2007). Flow in games (and everything else). *Communications of the ACM* 50(4): 31–34.

Cowley E. (2012). As a backdrop, part of the plot, or a goal in a game: The ubiquitous product placement. In Shrum L. J. (ed.). *The Psychology of Entertainment Media: Blurring the Lines between Entertainment and Persuasion* (2nd ed., pp. 37–63). New York: Taylor and Francis.

Cowley, B., Charles, D. Black, M., and Hickey, R. (2008). Toward an understanding of flow in video games. *Computers in Entertainment* 6(2): 27 pages.

Csikszentmihalyi, M. (1990). *Flow: The Psychology of Optimal Experience.* New York: HarperCollins.

Dunn, J. (2024, January 4). Day 5: The magic of losing yourself in a task. *The New York Times.* https://www.nytimes.com/2024/01/04/well/mind/energy-challenge-flow-focus.html

Gilbert, D. (2007). *Stumbling on Happiness.* New York: Vintage Books.

Grant, A. (2021, December 3). There's a name for the blah you're feeling: It's called languishing. *The New York Times.* https://www.nytimes.com/2021/04/19/well/mind/covid-mental-health-languishing.html

Grant, A. (2023). *You are not a machine.* LinkedIn. https://www.linkedin.com/feed/update/urn:li:activity:7091430191561879553/

Harris, D. J., Vine, S. J., and Wilson, M. R. (2017). Is flow really effortless? The complex role of effortful attention. *Sport, Exercise, and Performance Psychology* 6(1): 103–114.

Hurtado, T. (2023, November 30). *Living Your Own Life Agenda: Leisure.* University of Utah Health. https://uofuhealth.utah.edu/notes/2023/11/living-your-own-life-agenda-leisure

Iso-Ahola, S. (1979). Basic dimensions of definitions of leisure. *Journal of Leisure Research* 11: 28–39.

Jackson, S. A. and Csikszentmihalyi, M. (1999). *Flow in Sports: The Keys to Optimal Experiences and Performances.* Human Kinetics Books.

Jackson, S. A. and Roberts, G. C. (1992). Positive performance states of athletes: Toward a conceptual understanding of peak performance. *The Sports Psychologist* 6(2): 156–171.

Jin, S. A. (2012). Toward integrative models of flow: Effects of performance, skill, challenge, playfulness, and presence on flow in video games. *Journal of Broadcasting and Electronic Media* 56(2): 169–186.

Keller, J. and Landhäußer, A. (2012). The flow model revisited. In S. Engeser (ed.), *Advances in Flow Research* (pp. 51–64). New York: Springer.

Ledecky, K. (2020, July 2). *Tokyo, 2020ne here we come!* Facebook. https://www.facebook.com/KatieLedecky/posts/tokyo-2020ne-here-we-come-the-tyr-sport-usa-venzo-is-out-today-tyrvenzo-usa-batt/3311944378824531/

Linn, J. (2024, March 1). LeBron James' viral statement after lakers vs. clippers. *Sports Illustrated.* https://www.si.com/nba/clippers/news/lebron-james-viral-statement-after-lakers-vs-clippers

Mannell, R. C. (1984). A psychology for leisure research. *Society and Leisure* 7(1): 13–21.

Morrison, D. (2022, April 21). John Calipari quotes to inspire and entertain basketball fans. *On3.* https://www.on3.com/news/john-calipari-quotes-to-inspire-and-entertain-basketball-fans/

Nakamura, J. and Csikszentmihalyi, M. (2002). The concept of flow. In C. R. Snyder and S. J. Lopez (eds.). *Handbook of Positive Psychology* (pp. 89–105). Oxford University Press.

Neulinger, J. (1974). *The Psychology of Leisure: Research Approaches to the Study of Leisure.* Springfield, IL: Charles C. Thomas.

Neulinger, J. (1981). *The Psychology of Leisure* (2nd ed.). Springfield, IL: Charles C. Thomas.

Nicholls A. R., Perry J. L., Jones L., Sanctuary C., Carson F., Clough P. J. (2015). The mediating role of mental toughness in sport. *The Journal of Sports Medicine and Physical Fitness* 55(7–8): 824–834.

Nunley, K. (2024, January 27). 23 *Lebron James quotes: Lessons in failure, family, and grit. Home School Hoop.* https://homeschoolhoop.com/lebron-james-quotes/

Perkins, K. and Nakamura, J. (2012). Flow and leisure. In *Positive Leisure Science: From Subjective Experience to Social Contexts* (pp. 141–157). Dordrecht: Springer Netherlands.

Primeau, L. A. (1996). Work and leisure: Transcending the dichotomy. *American Journal of Occupational Therapy* 50: 569–577.

Shaw, E. (2016). Getty Images. https://www.nytimes.com/2016/11/09/sports/basketball/stephen-curry-golden-state-warriors-3-pointers.html

Stampone, A. (2019, August 27). 16 inspiring quotes from U.S. open tennis legend Arthur Ashe. *Entrepreneur.* https://www.entrepreneur.com/business-news/16-inspiring-quotes-from-us-open-tennis-legend-arthur-ashe/338541

Stroupe, B. (2022, January 26). *Heart rate during game and my heartratewatching the game.* Twitter. https://twitter.com/bobbystroupe/status/1486339443606925321

Tinsley, H. E. and Tinsley, D. J. (1986). A theory of the attributes, benefits, and causes of leisure experience. *Leisure Sciences* 8(1): 1–45.

Vaughn, D., Best, R., and Vieira, R. (2017, November 23). *Flow experience and sports products.* University of Oregon Lundquist College of Business. https://business.uoregon.edu/news/flow-experience-and-sports-products

Watkins Ross. *Setting Olympic sized goals to achieve financial success.* https://watkinsross.com/articles/2021-07-20-setting-olympic-sized-goals-to-achieve-financialsuccess/#:~:text=Swimmer%20Jessica%20Hardy%20says%2C%20%E2%80%9CMy,success%20doesn't

6

The Future of Flow in the Digital Society

In the three decades since Mihaly's seminal book, so much of human attention and consciousness has shifted from the physical world to the digital world – profoundly changing the way we spend our time, think, behave, communicate, collaborate, work, and play. Given that flow takes place depending on where we spend our time and attention, the digital world has the potential to be flow's greatest enabler, as well as its biggest obstacle. The internet, in three short decades of popular existence, has become the primary hub for our news, entertainment, research, socializing, and getting work done. Let's rewind a few decades. In the 1980s for example, I would get most of my news from one or two sources (e.g., my local newspaper and *60 Minutes*), and only interact with people I was physically with, except for a phone call or two if I had the time. There was far more mental down time, with fewer sources of available stimulation at my disposal at any given moment.

Now, let's take a typical day in today's digitally enabled society. Many of us wake up and immediately check our phones, where some version of the following awaits us: work emails, texts from friends, notifications from all of our social media platforms (e.g., Instagram, TikTok, X), breaking news headlines from every source we've ever given our email. We could easily keep our minds occupied on our phones for every waking second of the day if we didn't have other responsibilities. If we have a question about anything whatsoever, Wikipedia, Google, and countless other sources are competing to be the first source we use to get the

Flow 2.0: Optimal Experience in a Complex World. Honoring Mihaly Csikszentmihalyi's Legacy, First Edition. Stewart I. Donaldson and Matthew Dubin.
© 2025 John Wiley & Sons Ltd. Published 2025 by John Wiley & Sons Ltd.

answer. On YouTube, we can watch hours upon hours of videos on the exact topic that excites us at any given moment, where you could teach yourself to play the guitar, hang drywall, or write a good résumé, and then reward yourself with hours of highlights of the 1990s Michael Jordan Bulls games. It can also act as a supplement for other experiences, where you can finish an episode of your favorite show and then hop online for instant reactions and fan theories on Reddit. Perhaps most commonly, however, is the mindless scroll, where we hop on a social media platform and look at hundreds of posts in succession, an activity that can move from engaging to numbing in a hurry if we're not careful.

These online experiences are so universally ubiquitous now, we really forget how new it is – and that people as young as 30 grew up with the long static-tone of an internet dial-up. It reminds me of watching any footage or shows from the 1950s or 1960s, where every single person or character was smoking a cigarette and would go through pack after pack in succession without a second thoughts about the potential ramifications. Now, when you see photos of any major sporting event, concert, or cultural moment, the majority of people will have their phones up, viewing the experience through the digital screens to ultimately share online. The photo in Figure 6.1 went viral in 2015, showing a phoneless older lady soaking in an experience, surrounded by a sea of mobile devices during the Boston red carpet premiere of the film *Black Mass*.

Figure 6.1 The 2015 Boston red carpet premiere of the film *Black Mass*. *Source:* John Blanding/The Boston Globe/Getty Images.

We eventually learned about the devastating health consequences of cigarettes, and they gradually stopped showing up between people's fingertips as establishments began to designate no-smoking areas – then smoking areas, then, increasingly, no smoking permitted. Where there used to be a cigarette, we now hold our phones, addicted to the dopamine hits in the same way we used to be addicted to nicotine. The long-term effects of "phone addiction" are still unfolding, and we now have the term *nomophobia* to describe the fear of being without our mobile devices.

From a flow perspective, this means there's never been an easier way to instantly engage your mind. However, engaging your mind does not necessarily equate to being in flow – a holistic, meaningful experience that utilizes your skills to match a given challenge. Most activities we interact with have a natural end point: An episode of a show ends after 30 or 60 minutes, a puzzle is complete when there are no more pieces to fit, the cookies are done when they come out of the oven. By contrast, the digital universe is an endless playground, with information and content forever expanding like the physical universe. Engaging in a healthy relationship with the digital world requires discipline and intentionality. A lot has been discussed about limiting the amount of time we spend on our phones and on the internet, which is definitely important, but less attention is spent on the quality of our online experiences. A 30-minute Instagram scroll vs. spending 30 minutes learning Spanish on Duolingo should not be seen as equivalent: One experience often leads to feelings of insecurity, anxiety, and fatigue, while the other enables us to enhance our skills, achieve goals, and expand the self.

While scrolling can be a relaxing way to unwind or pass the time in line at Starbucks, it shouldn't be the predominant method with which we use our devices. The more we can unlock our phone for a specific purpose: to learn, communicate, play a game, etc., the more likely it is that its use will lead to flow. Decreasing the quantity and increasing the quality of our consumption will lead to a more flow-conducive relationship with our devices.

Although increasing the quality of consumption can enhance experience when we are actually attending to a single activity or task, this doesn't change the fact that our sense of time confetti will continue to persist into the near future. Time confetti, where our time and attention are broken up into thousands of fragments (like pieces of confetti) caused by (mostly digital) distractions, is a fact of life that cannot be "fixed" with a simple tweak. Instead of trying to eliminate all distraction, which is nearly impossible, it is perhaps more adaptive to improve our relationship with distraction. British author and journalist Oliver Burkeman, author of the book *Four Thousand Weeks: Time Management for Mortals,* has a fresh perspective on how to frame distraction (Burkeman 2021). On a 2024 podcast episode of *Plain English* with *Atlantic* journalist and author Derek Thompson, he discusses the challenge of trying to deeply focus and avoid context switching:

> *I think that the subtle problem that underlies all of this is that the more you go through your day with a very clear conceptual intellectual plan for how it should go, for what the boundaries of your time are, for what you're doing for the next three hours, and what will be a problem if you get interrupted or blown off course, the more you bring that to your day, the worse it is when you are interrupted.*
>
> *(Thompson 2024, 00:10:20)*

He suggests that we change our relationship with interruptions, as opposed to seeing them as an enemy that completely derails of our day. For example, if you are able to work from home and then your child bursts into your office to tell you about her day at school when you are trying to focus on a work task, it can be quite frustrating in the moment.

In Dubin's (2018) dissertation study, a consistent pattern in the responses of workers when asked about their flow experiences at work was that they found unwanted interruptions to be quite irritating. Burkeman's point, however, is that not all interruptions should be viewed the same way, and we can end up missing some of life's organic, beautiful moments if we are too rigid about avoiding interruption. Knowing interruption is a fact of life, it is perhaps a more sustainable strategy to evaluate interruptions as they come, and for certain ones – like our child coming to tell us about her school day – we should lean into the interruption (if we can), give our full attention to it, and then return to our task. In particular cases, the interruption itself could be its own source of joy and flow, but only if we are open to viewing it as such. The podcast episode references this quote from C.S. Lewis: "The great thing, if one can, is to stop regarding all the unpleasant things as interruptions of one's 'own,' or 'real' life. The truth is of course that what one calls the interruptions are precisely one's real life – the life God is sending one day by day" (Thompson 2024).

Flow and Artificial Intelligence

Up to this point, we have delineated between the physical world and the digital world as two separate states of experience. However, with the exponential advancement of artificial intelligence, virtual reality, and augmented reality, the fundamental nature of human experience itself may well likely change, blending the physical and digital worlds into something entirely new. We have only scratched the surface of the capabilities of these technologies. In AI, the most popular platform to be released is ChatGPT, a chatbot using a large language model (LLM) that can take any prompt and provide a detailed, instantaneous response. It can write your next essay and plan your next trip in less than 10 seconds. It removes the challenge almost completely from a myriad of tasks that used to require substantial skill. As AI technology develops, its capabilities will far exceed that of the human mind, with existential fear that the majority of our jobs will be rendered meaningless and, eventually, humanity will lose control of AI. Correctly harnessing the power of AI for good will be one of the defining objectives of our time. The interplay between humans and AI will also have far-reaching ramifications for the types of flow experiences that we will have in the near future. Using AI effectively will require a whole new host of skills, and those who develop these skills to meet the fresh demands that AI presents will likely find themselves operating more efficiently and performing at a higher level. AI in customer service, for example, is currently equipped to handle repetitive, mundane tasks, where chatbots can reply to customer questions and provide answers to cut-and-dry questions.

In an ideal world, this would free up our time to engage in more complex tasks that would be more likely to enable flow, where we can be more creative and energized. Another current example is that AI can currently sift through thousands of resumes for a job to identify the most qualified candidates, freeing up a recruiter to focus on the more nuanced aspects of selecting the best person for the job. The main drawback in the short-term as it relates to AI pertains to the flow characteristic of perceived control over the flow task. When we are making a cookie recipe, for example, we have full control over how much flour, sugar, and butter we mix together. When painting, we have full control over the color and direction of each brush stroke. With AI tools, however, part of the appeal is naturally relinquishing control over tasks that the technology can perform more efficiently and/or effectively. It stands to reason that every year the technology advances, we will naturally give up more and more control over tasks we used to do manually in favor of AI support. Taken to an extreme, we will find ourselves not in control of our daily experience, and perhaps even our consciousness, if we allow AI to become too pervasive of an element in our lives. For example, AI has the capacity to create *digital twins* – "a digital representation of something that exists in physical reality" (Cotriss 2022).

Jordan Richard Schoenherr, the assistant professor of psychology at Concordia University in Canada, says:

> *As a copy of a person, a digital twin would – ideally – make the same decisions that you would make if you were presented with the same materials. While we might tend to assume that we are special and unique, with a sufficient amount of information, artificial intelligence (AI) can make many inferences about our personalities, social behaviour and purchasing decisions.*
>
> *(Schoenherr 2022)*

Wow, and also, yikes.

A future where we all have digital twins whom we delegate thoughts, ideas, questions, and decisions to would fundamentally change human experience and greatly inhibit the capacity for flow that stems from the mind. Over the coming decades, there will be ample opportunity for us to have richer flow experiences as we become accustomed to knowing where, when, and how to use AI tools for our benefit. If not regulated properly, however, we will be muting and perhaps relinquishing the richness of human experience – the mental struggle that leads to a great idea, the connection and wisdom that comes from learning from other people – in favor of tools that we think "can do it for us." AI can provide a destination, but life – and flow – is about the messy, complex journey.

Moving forward, human experience will take place in three domains: the physical world, the digital world, and physical-digital hybrid. The first *homo sapiens* (modern human) evolved 200,000–300,000 years ago, and flow took place in the physical world until the twenty-first century. Our brains evolved to survive and thrive in the physical world. Now, many of us spend the majority of our waking hours in the digital world, where humanity has only two decades of experience. It is no wonder why anxiety is at record levels, especially among teenagers. We have fundamentally altered the human experience and expect ourselves to be able to handle it seamlessly, an impossible task when we zoom out. Mihaly's first book is called *Beyond Boredom and Anxiety* (1975) since optimal experience took place when the equilibrium between skill and challenge would allow us to transcend boredom and avoid anxiety.

Full access to the digital world has seemed to completely eradicate boredom from the human experience, since we can occupy our minds and avoid our inner thoughts whenever we'd like. However, the price we seem to pay for trading in boredom is an influx of anxiety with compounding interest, since we have not yet developed the cognitive, emotional, and psychological skills to handle the interpersonal and political challenges that the digital world presents. The future of flow depends on investing resources to train our minds, especially young people who are more vulnerable, to engage in the digital world in a healthier way. Furthermore, we must provide inner guardrails to operate in this world, knowing our personal boundaries, avoiding over consumption, and engaging in the content that enriches our souls.

Overflow: Mitigating a Future of Digital Flow Addiction and Loneliness

When considering the future of flow, we cannot assume that its presence is inherently positive (Table 6.1). "Like other forms of energy, from fire to nuclear fission, it [flow] can be used for both positive and

Table 6.1 The dark side of flow's characteristics.

Flow characteristics	The dark sides of flow characteristics
Loss of self-reflection	Neglecting further goals and values (of others)
Exclusive concentration on the task at hand	Narrowed focus of attention excluding additional information
High control, absence of anxiety	Overestimation of one's abilities, unrealistic optimism
Distortion of time	Neglecting temporal information although it is relevant

Source: Zimanyi and Schüler (2021) and Schüler (2012).

destructive ends" (Csikszentmihalyi and Rathunde 1993, p. 91). Considering that flow is complete immersion in a task where we lose our sense of self-awareness, it stands to reason that this immersion would not always be applied in an adaptive way (Zimanyi and Schüler 2021). For example, I would spend hours playing video games in high school which would cause me to procrastinate on my homework, meaning I wouldn't get enough sleep for the next school day. Therefore, the intrinsic enjoyment felt while playing video games came at the expense of other important goals. In a work context, a manager may be in flow leading a meeting, becoming so engrossed in the content they are sharing that they neglect to involve others, hampering their ability to experience flow along with them. As Mihaly said, "When a person becomes so dependent on the ability to control an enjoyable activity that he cannot pay attention to anything else, then he loses the ultimate control: the freedom to determine the contents of consciousness. Thus, enjoyable activities that produce flow have a potentially negative aspect" (Csikszentmihalyi 1990, p. 62).

The flow experience can be so intoxicating that it has the potential to lead to addictive behavior. The *International Classification of Diseases* (ICD 10, World Health Organization 1994, as cited in Schüler 2021) defines addiction as "the use of a substance takes on a much higher priority for a given individual than other behaviors that once had greater value." When we experience flow, we often seek to replicate the experience again and again, which can lead to addictive tendencies.

Flow has been linked to addictive behavior in three domains: computer/video games, exercising, and internet use. In a 2008 study, Thatcher and his colleagues looked at the relationship between the flow state and problematic internet use, which was defined as the "use of the Internet that creates psychological, social, school, and/or work difficulties in a person's life" (Beard and Wolf 2001, p. 378). They found that the stronger the participants' experience of flow, the more significant increase there was in their problematic internet use. In the last 17 years, the internet has become far more complex, with far more sites, videos, blogs, discussion forums, and other avenues to engage. The potential for overflow will only become more prevalent, especially as the lines between the physical and digital worlds become more intertwined. For example, the very first version of the Apple Vision Pro was released in 2024 (Figure 6.2), which Apple says, "seamlessly blends digital content with your physical space."

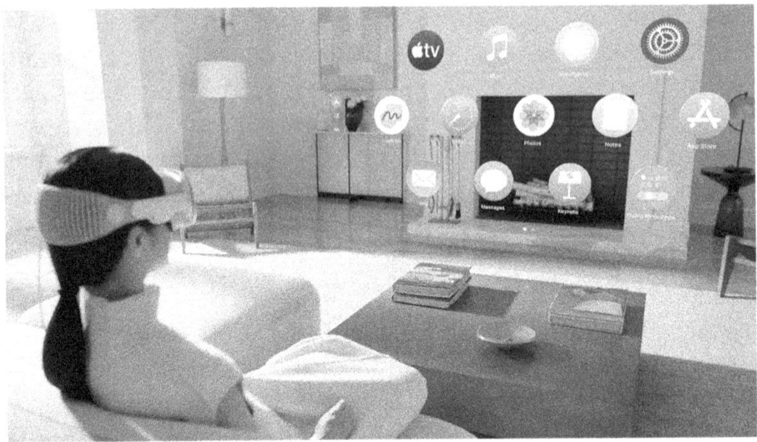

Figure 6.2 Apple Vision Pro. *Source:* RTLY / https://www.rlty.live/post/apple-vision-pro-and-spatial-computing-what-does-it-mean-for-rlty/ last accessed March 25, 2024.

As we can see in Figure 6.2, our technological future in the near term may very well involve wearing some sort of headset that fundamentally changes our relationship with the physical world, and thus other people, even if we can technically still see our physical world through the headset. Creating an additional barrier to interacting with others, while increasing the frequency and intensity of our engagement with the digital world, may very well lead to a future where flow becomes a largely individual, digitally driven experience.

Flow in the Future: The Balance of Social Interaction in the Digital and Physical Worlds

In February 2024, Derek Thompson wrote an article for *The Atlantic* called "Why Americans Suddenly Stopped Hanging Out." In the article, he shares a striking statistic from the *American Time Use Survey*: From 2003 to 2022, American adults have reduced the amount they socialize face-to-face by 30%, and the decline is even steeper for teenagers (50%). While the impact of the COVID-19 pandemic is definitely a factor, the stat indicates these trends have been going on for far longer, and largely are tied to the rise of the internet in everyone's homes and devices. For teenagers especially, the use of online spaces to socialize and interact with others has largely replaced meeting in-person and interacting face-to-face. As digital experiences continue to become even more prevalent and immersive, individuals seeking flow through the digital world will likely far outweigh flow experiences in the physical world.

If this is the case, collective flow experiences (as described in Chapter 3) will precipitously decline as well. This would have a continued detrimental effect on our mental health. In 2023, Gallup reported that the percentage of US adults who have been diagnosed with depression at some point in their lifetime was 29%, almost 10% higher than 2015 (Witters 2023). Researchers at Harvard conducted a study where they tracked the lives of 724 men for 75 years, and the most essential factor for sustained happiness is quality relationships. “The lesson that came from tens of thousands of pages of that research was that good relationships keep us happier and healthier,” said Dr. Robert Waldinger, the psychiatrist and director of the study (Oppong 2019).

Mihaly says, “People are more happy, alert, and cheerful if there are others present, compared to how they feel alone, whether they are working on an assembly line or watching television” (Csikszentmihalyi 1990, p. 168). From a flow perspective, the question then becomes: How do we build, nurture, and sustain quality social relationships if we are spending more time alone in a digital world? The most obvious and straightforward answer is to make sure we continue to carve out time for social interaction in the physical world, but it will not be so simple. The digital world will only become more convenient and addicting, not to mention the continued development of the metaverse. Mark Zuckerberg, the founder of Facebook, so deeply believes in the future of the metaverse that he rebranded his company to be called Meta. The website leans into social connection aspect of this world, with two headlines being:

1) We believe in the future of connection in the metaverse.
2) The metaverse provides new ways to connect and share new experiences.

So, what is the metaverse, exactly? According to Koss, “The metaverse refers to an immersive and persistent three-dimensional virtual realm, shared with many users, that spans various digital platforms and merges with the physical world, where people can shop, work, play, and hang out together in real time” (Koss 2022). Therefore, instead of a virtual meeting on Zoom, where each of us show up in our physical space as two-dimensional boxes on a screen, we would all have a digital avatar and share a 3-D digital space

Figure 6.3 Meeting in the metaverse, avatar style. *Source:* McMahon (2023)/ LineZero Corp.

together, perhaps sitting at a table together and closely replicating the experience of an in-person meeting (Figure 6.3).

These types of digital environments could reintroduce factors that somewhat replicate physical interaction, potentially increasing the probability of a collective flow experience: We could again be in three-dimensional space and could have more in-rhythm conversations without the standard choppiness and interruptions that often result from boxes in a screen. This would enable several of the characteristics of group flow, such as close listening, being more familiar with each other's style and ticks, being able to fully concentrate on one another, and blending egos if we feel immersed in a shared space.

Advances in AI and metaverse technology will, therefore, be more effective at enabling collective flow than our current, two-dimensional digital environments, but the fear is that they will progress to such an extent that no one would feel the need to share an actual physical space, due to the convenience and ease of shared digital space.

In a 2023 study by Kroencke et al. of 3,000 college students, effects of different types of interactions were examined: face-to-face, computer-mediated communication, and mixed episodes (face-to-face and computer-mediated). They found that face-to-face interactions and mixed episodes were related to the highest levels of well-being, with computer-mediated communication being related to lower levels of well-being. During in-person interaction, we can more easily pick up on nonverbal cues and body language, make eye contact, better understand the intent behind someone's words, and work through potential disagreements. Even the act of physical touch can promote more quality interactions. Schroeder et al. (2019) at the University of Chicago and Harvard found that the simple act of shaking hands before a negotiation led to more cooperative behavior, higher levels of joint outcomes, more transparency on trade-off issues, and a higher likelihood of the negotiators telling the truth. The future of collective flow will therefore heavily rely on two factors: whether technological advances can largely replicate the quality of in-person interactions in digital settings (mainly out of our personal control, at least for most of us), and intentionally making time for in-person interaction in a shared physical space (mostly within our control).

In modern society, much of in-person interaction takes place in what is called a *third place*, a social environment that is separate from our two main social places: home (first) and work (second). Third places are environments where we are intrinsically motivated to be there, with no external obligations for productivity or financial gain. In his book *The Great Good Place* written in 1989 (only a year before *Flow* was released), author Ray Oldenburg coined the term and made the case that third places are essential for a high-functioning society where civility, engagement, community, and creativity can thrive. Examples of third places include cafes, bars, malls. restaurants, churches, community centers, gyms, parks, theaters – really, any environment that provides a sense of place on neutral territory with no requirement to be there, and where conversation is an inherent element in the experience. Simply put, Oldenburg says, "Your third place is where you relax in public."

Howard Schultz (2008), the CEO of Starbucks, describes the ubiquitous coffee shop as such: "We are the third place in the lives of millions of our customers. We are the coffee that brings people together every day around the world to foster conversation and community." Collective flow thrives in third places, where people can be fully themselves, more vulnerable, and there to converse for intrinsic reasons.

Since Oldenburg's ideas entered the public domain, researchers have naturally begun to explore the possibility of virtual third places. While Oldenburg has maintained that third places should be in-person interactions where people meet face to face, Allucquere Rosanne Stone (1991) defines online community as "social spaces in which people still meet face-to-face, but under new definitions of both 'meet' and 'face'."

In the 1.0 version of the internet, when Stone wrote those words, online communities largely consisted of message boards where people could find a group of people with shared interests and discuss thoughts, ideas, and questions in the written form. The future of digital third places may very well include virtual versions of physical third places (e.g., Starbucks is apparently working on a virtual third place in the metaverse). For collective flow to thrive in the future, virtual third places must greatly improve and serve as a supplement, but not a replacement, for physical third places.

An Optimal Future for Optimal Experience

In the original flow studies, the flow "domains" that were investigated in the 1970s were bound to the physical world: Surgeons, dancers, rock climbers, painters. This chapter has focused on the transition to the digital world of the present day, engaging in activities, content, or connection through a two-dimensional screen, and also looking into the future of the digital world – likely to be powered by AI and the metaverse – and its potential impact on the human experience through a flow lens. While the roadblocks and pitfalls of flow have swelled, the digital world as a supplement to the physical world has also created an abundance of new opportunities for flow – which will continue to exponentially increase. The never-ending stream of stimulation has basically eradicated the feeling of sitting alone with our thoughts that would often lead to psychic entropy:

> *Contrary to what we tend to assume, the normal state of the mind is chaos. Without training, and without an object in the external world that demands attention, people are unable to focus their thoughts for more than a few minutes at a time...People are naturally eager to fill their minds with whatever information is readily available. As long as it distracts attention from turning inward and dwelling on negative feelings.*
>
> *(Csikszentmihalyi 1990, p. 119)*

Our phones provide a 24-hour source of readily available information that is eager, and financially motivated, to distract us from our inner thoughts and feelings. This digital stimulation also provides instant gratification, leading to potentially addictive behavior. With stimulation readily available at times, we have nearly eliminated boredom from the human experience. On the surface, this doesn't seem like a bad thing – almost none of us would *choose* boredom over engagement, and flow in many ways is the antithesis of boredom. Here lies a great paradox that will have major implications in the quality of flow experiences we enjoy in the future. The experience of boredom may very well lead to higher-quality, more meaningful flow experiences, where we are not only engaged but also able to be more creative and fulfilled.

In one study examining boredom, the authors separated participants into two groups: One group completed a "boring" task (sorting a bowl of beans by color), and the other group was assigned to complete a more interesting craft activity. The group that first completed the boring task was later more productive on an idea-generating activity than the group that first completed the interesting task (Park et al. 2019). In another study (Gasper and Middlewood 2014), the authors had participants watch different video clips that elicited different emotions – such as boredom, relaxation, or elation. Afterward, participants were asked to think of different vocabulary words when asked to think of vehicles. Participants who were in the "relaxed" or "elated" conditions most often said "car," whereas participants in the boredom condition would often come up with more creative words (one participant saying *camel*, for example).

When our brain is allowed those quiet moments to wander, it often wanders toward the future, helping us set future personal goals, or what researchers call *autobiographical planning* (Baird et al. 2011). Boredom also allows us time to assess our current circumstances, thinking more deeply about shifts we may want to make to enhance our life experience more holistically, whether we realize that our job isn't challenging or that we aren't nurturing our friendships enough with people we deeply care about.

This doesn't mean that we must seek out experiences of boredom in an intentional way, but instead to not wholly avoid them at every opportunity. For example, we don't need to look at our phones when in line at a coffee shop, waiting at a crosswalk, or passing the time when waiting for a friend to arrive who is running late. Life will naturally provide those moments, and it will require immense discipline to not instinctively try and distract our minds when they arise.

Neil Gaiman, a popular and prolific English novelist, has this advice for aspiring writers:

> *Ideas come from daydreaming. They come from drifting. The trouble with these days is that it's really hard to get bored. I have 2.4 million people on Twitter who will entertain me at any moment…it's really hard to get bored. I'm much better at putting my phone away, going for boring walks, actually trying to find the space to get bored in. That's what I've started saying to people who say, "I want to be a great writer," I say, "great, get bored."*
>
> *(Newport 2016)*

The present and near future, therefore, will be constantly filled with transitory microflow experiences – small moments of deep engagement in digital experiences that aren't ultimately meaningful, fulfilling, or productive. To have the flow experiences that ultimately transform the self, allowing moments of boredom may be an important key. It is in these moments where we can reflect on our past, consider the future, and ultimately carve out a path toward self-actualization. "A person who has achieved control over psychic energy and has invested it in consciously chosen goals cannot help but grow into a more complex being. By stretching skills, by reaching toward higher challenges, such a person becomes an increasingly extraordinary individual" (Csikszentmihalyi 1990). Mihaly's first book in 1975 was called *Beyond Boredom and Anxiety*, with flow being the desired sweet spot between these two undesirable emotions. Since then, anxiety rates have risen sharply, while the digital world can allow us to instantaneously escape boredom at any moment.

James Danckert, a cognitive neuroscientist at the University of Waterloo and co-author of *Out of My Skull: The Psychology of Boredom*, discusses how reflexively checking our phones can create a vicious cycle since it's not a particularly meaningful experience, meaning another bout of boredom is right round the corner (Danckert 2023). He suggests that we be more mindful about the signal that boredom is sending us: What would be a more meaningful use of our time? What are our core values, goals, or priorities?

The amount of flow experiences available to us is now reminiscent of a giant grocery store, with 25 brands of peanut butter to choose from, 20 brands of jelly, and 40 types of bread. As psychologist Barry Schwartz famously told us in *The Paradox of Choice* (2016), an overabundance of choices leads to greater anxiety and frustration. When it comes to choosing the right flow experiences in our future, the ones that are truly meaningful, challenging, and self-expanding, the capacity for boredom may be the prerequisite that enables us to take the time to make proactive flow decisions and not simply react to whatever hollow stimuli the digital world is offering on that particular day.

References

Apple Vision Pro. (2024). https://www.apple.com/apple-vision-pro/

Baird, B., Smallwood, J., and Schooler, J. W. (2011). Back to the future: Autobiographical planning and the functionality of mind-wandering. *Consciousness and Cognition: An International Journal* 20(4), 1604–1611.

Beard, K. W. and Wolf, E. M. (2001). Modification in the proposed diagnostic criteria for internet addiction. *Cyberpsychology and Behavior* 4(3), 377–383.

Blanding, J. (2015). Getty Image. The Boston Globe.

Burkeman, O. (2021). *Four Thousand Weeks: Time Management for Mortals*. Farrar, Straus and Giroux.

Cotriss, D. (2022, October 31). *How AI is supercharging digital twins*. Nasdaq. https://www.nasdaq.com/articles/how-ai-is-supercharging-digital-twins

Csikszentmihalyi, M. (1975). *Beyond Boredom and Anxiety*. San Francisco: Jossey-Bass.

Csikszentmihalyi, M. (1990). *Flow: The Psychology of Optimal Experience*. New York: HarperCollins.

Csikszentmihalyi, M. and Rathunde, K. (1993). The measurement of flow in everyday life: Toward a theory of emergent motivation. *Nebraska Symposium on Motivation* 40: 57–97.

Danckert, J. (2023, August 8). *James Danckert on the (Important) Role of Boredom in Our Lives*. University of Waterloo. https://uwaterloo.ca/arts/news/james-danckert-important-role-boredom-our-lives

Dubin, M. (2018). *Experiencing Flow at Work as a Digital Native in an Accelerated Knowledge Economy*. Doctoral dissertation. Claremont, CA: Claremont Graduate University.

Gasper, K. and Middlewood, B. L. (2014). Approaching novel thoughts: Understanding why elation and boredom promote associative thought more than distress and relaxation. *Journal of Experimental Social Psychology* 52: 50–57.

ICD-10. World Health Organization. (1994). *International Statistical Classification of Diseases and Related Health Problems*. ICD-10. Genève: World Health Organization.

Koss, H. (2022, October 6). What is the metaverse, really? *Builtin*. https://builtin.com/media-gaming/what-is-metaverse

Kroencke, L., Harari, G. M., Back, M. D., and Wagner, J. (2023). Well-being in social interactions: Examining personality-situation dynamics in face-to-face and computer-mediated communication. *Journal of Personality and Social Psychology* 124(2): 437–460.

McMahon, J. (2023, August, 31). What are the meetings in the metaverse? The future of virtual office. *Linezero*. https://www.linezero.com/blog/what-are-the-meetings-in-the-metaverse

Meta. 2024. https://about.meta.com/

Newport, C. (2016, November 11). Neil Gaiman's advice to writers: Get bored. *Cal Newport*. https://calnewport.com/neil-gaimans-advice-to-writers-get-bored/

Oldenburg, R. (1989). *The Great Good Place*. New York: Paragon House.

Oppong, T. (2019, October 18). *Good social relationships are the most consistent predictor of a happy life*. Thrive Global. https://community.thriveglobal.com/relationships-happiness-well-being-life-lessons/

Park, G., Lim, B. C., and Oh, H. S. (2019). Why being bored might not be a bad thing after all. *Academy of Management* 5(1).

RLTY. (2023, August 30. *Apple vision pro and spatial computing: What does it mean for RLTY?* https://www.rlty.live/post/apple-vision-pro-and-spatial-computing-what-does-it-mean-for-rlty

Schoenherr, J. R. (2022, July 22). Digital doubles: In the future, virtual versions of ourselves could predict our behaviour. *The Conversation*. https://theconversation.com/digital-doubles-in-the-future-virtual-versions-of-ourselves-could-predict-our-behaviour-186627

Schroeder, J., Risen, J. L., Gino, F., and Norton, M. I. (2019). Handshaking promotes deal-making by signaling cooperative intent. *Journal of Personality and Social Psychology* 116(5): 743–768.

Schüler, J. (2012). The dark side of the moon. In S. Engeser (ed.), *Advances in flow Research* (pp. 123–137). Springer Science + Business Media.

Schultz, H. (2008, February 24). *Howard Schultz communication transformation agenda communication #8*. Starbucks Stories and News. https://stories.starbucks.com/press/2008/howard-schultz-transformation-agenda-communication-8/

Schwartz, B. (2016). *The Paradox of Choice*. ECCO Press.

Stone, A. R. (1991). Will the real body please stand up? In M. Benedikt (ed.). *Cyberspace: First Steps,* Cambridge, MA: MIT Press.

Thatcher, A., Wretschko, G., and Fridjhon, P. (2008). Online flow experiences, problematic internet use and internet procrastination. *Computers in human behavior* 24(5): 2236–2254.

Thompson, D. (2024, February 14). Why Americans suddenly stopped hanging out. *The Atlantic*. https://www.theatlantic.com/ideas/archive/2024/02/america-decline-hanging-out/677451/

Thompson, D. (host). (2024, January 9). The dark side of the obsession with focus. *Plain English*. Audio podcast. January 9; 45 min, 34 sec.

Witters, D. (2023, May 17). *U.S. depression rates reach new highs*. Gallup. Retrieved from https://news.gallup.com/poll/505745/depression-rates-reach-new-highs.aspx

Zimanyi, Z. and Schüler, J. (2021). The dark side of the moon. In C. Peifer and S. Engeser (eds.). *Advances in Flow Research* (pp. 171–190). Springer Nature Switzerland AG.

Part III

Summing Up and Conclusions

7

What Mihaly's Insights Mean for Our Lives

Human Flourishing, Well-Being, and Positive Functioning in the Years Ahead

This chapter attempts to blend the personal and professional insights that Mihaly has passed on to us in our personal interactions with him over many years, his teaching and mentoring, his profound scholarship and writing, and as a role model of kindness and compassion for humankind. Our hope is that by sharing these nuggets you will be inspired to read more of his original work, and to enrich your life by following some of his ideas about how to live the good life and pursue good work, human flourishing, well-being, and positive functioning.

The Legacy He Wanted to Leave: Positive Psychology

We (Stewart and Mihaly) would talk with Mihaly for hours about how positive psychology might someday be able to help turn the world's attention away from mostly focusing on the worst of humankind and the destruction of the planet, toward a more hopeful and balanced view that also highlights and celebrates strengths (in addition to weaknesses), assets (in addition to deficits), human flourishing (instead of death, destruction, and despair), and the overall topic of focusing on what makes life worth living. One of his most profound ideas that he wanted me (Stewart) to convey to prospective positive psychology students and other professionals who want to join the positive psychology community was: Their own lives, and the lives of their loved ones, are likely to be greatly enriched if they join us in learning about and exploring the science and practice of positive

Flow 2.0: Optimal Experience in a Complex World. Honoring Mihaly Csikszentmihalyi's Legacy, First Edition. Stewart I. Donaldson and Matthew Dubin.
© 2025 John Wiley & Sons Ltd. Published 2025 by John Wiley & Sons Ltd.

Figure 7.1 Mihaly Csikszentmihalyi honored by Google on his 89th birthday.

psychology. Mihaly firmly believed that where we focus our attention and spend the major of our time and energy determines the quality of our lives.

> *Attention is like energy in that without it no work can be done, and in doing work is dissipated. We create ourselves by how we use this energy. Memories, thoughts and feelings are all shaped by how use it. And it is an energy under control, to do with as we please; hence attention is our most important tool in the task of improving the quality of experience.*
>
> *(Csikszentmihalyi 1990, p. 48)*

He highly encouraged us to focus our precious attention on understanding and applying the science of positive psychology. However, he often seemed very concerned that some who learn about the theories and ideas of positive psychology would lack the discipline to base their actions and applications in rigorous scientific evidence. That is, their enthusiasm for the concepts of positive psychology would get the better of them. This is why he put so much emphasis in his programs and courses on teaching positive psychology students about scientific research, evaluation, evidence-based interventions, and the value and rigor of the best peer-reviewed journals for our work. The research-based PhD and MA programs we developed together with Professor Jeanne Nakamura were heavily grounded in these ideas and values. Many of our alumni are now major contributors to the positive psychological science literature, and are leaders in both the science and evidence-informed practice of positive psychology.

One aspect of Mihaly's vision for his legacy was to build a community of positive psychology scholars and practitioners who shared his high standards and values. One of those values is "other people," and he strongly agreed with the phrase coined by positive psychology pioneer Christopher

Peterson: "Other people matter" (Donaldson & Donaldson 2018). In fact, he believed that caring for your own well-being, optimal experience, and positive functioning is important but incomplete; you also need to learn how to do it in way that enriches others.

> *The task is to learn how to enjoy everyday life without diminishing other people's chances of enjoying theirs.*
>
> *(Csikszentmihalyi 1990, p. 90)*

He also realized he could not build the science and practice of positive psychology he envisioned leaving to future generations alone. Even though leadership might not have been his natural strength or interest, he worked hard with his colleagues to inspire others to study positive psychology topics and build a scientific literature on human flourishing. It was clear he had succeeded when Donaldson and colleagues (2015) took stock of the first 15 years of the peer-reviewed literature linked to the vision for a science of positive psychology in their widely cited article "Happiness, Excellence, and Optimal Human Functioning Revisited: Examining the Peer-reviewed Literature linked to Positive Psychology." They found his call for a science of positive psychology was clearly answered with more than 1,300 peer-reviewed publications on positive psychology topics – and with more than 750 of these articles including empirical tests of positive psychology theories, principles, and interventions. It was found that well-being and positive functioning in schools, work, and life in general were among the most heavily investigated topics. Other popular topics included character strengths, hope, gratitude, resilience, and growth. Collectively, these scientific findings revealed that the science of positive psychology had become a growing sub-area within the broader discipline of psychology and was using the scientific methods of psychology to better understand well-being, excellence, and optimal human functioning.

Nearly 10 years later in 2023, this initial review was updated and expanded as an entry in the third edition of the *Encyclopedia of Mental Health* describing the state of the field he created and elaborating on some of its main findings:

- "More than two decades of peer-reviewed science supports the practice of positive psychology.
- "PERMA+4 provides an evidenced-based framework for guiding the assessment, development, and management of well-being and positive functioning.

- "Causal evidence supports that Positive Psychology Interventions (PPI) work on average, and work well under specific conditions.
- "The science and practice of positive psychology continues to grow and is being taught at universities and through professional associations across the world" (Donaldson et al. 2023, p. 79).

His bold vision of creating a positive psychology community had expanded throughout the world. While the early days of positive psychology were based in the US, Kim and colleagues (2018) in their seminal review "The International Landscape of Positive Psychology Research: A Systematic Review" showed that the science of positive psychology had spread throughout various regions of the world, and that the majority of scholarly contributions to positive psychology are now being carried out outside the United States.

Mihaly was instrumental in the establishment of The International Association of Positive Psychology (IPPA) in 2007. IPPA's mission is:

- To advance the scientific study and ethical application of positive psychology.
- To facilitate collaboration among researchers, teachers, students, and practitioners of positive psychology around the world and across academic disciplines.
- To share the findings of positive psychology with the broadest possible international audience.

I had the great pleasure of hosting as Congress Chair the IPPA 2013 World Congress of Positive Psychology with Mihaly and Professor Jeanne Nakamura in Los Angeles, CA, with some events on our campus at the Claremont Colleges. Mihaly was so excited to see this event come to his region of the country and home campus. He was especially thrilled for our positive psychology graduate students to present their research, and to meet and interact with many of the founders and leading researchers in the field. Once the 2013 World Congress was over, there seemed to be a great demand for more discussions and positive psychology conferences in the Western region of the United States. IPPA's mission was to hold future World Congresses in other cities across the world. This inspired Mihaly and me to establish the Western Positive Psychology Association (WPPA) and host annual conferences in the West and mostly on the Claremont Colleges campus. Our eighth annual WPPA conference (2024) was held at the University of New Mexico, and the ninth annual WPPA conference (2025) is scheduled to take place at Sacramento State University.

In addition to our community building work in the western US, a wide range of national and regional positive psychology professional associations, and university courses and degrees have been developed. He seemed so pleased with how his ideas and the global positive psychology community had grown much faster than he would have expected. That is, those initial ideas and bold vision for positive psychology had resulted in a robust community illustrated by the sample of professional associations, courses, and degrees displayed in Table 7.1.

Table 7.1 Illustrative sample of associations and degree programs by continent.

	Associations	Courses and Degrees
Europe	• European Network of Positive Psychology • German-Speaking Association of Positive Psychology (German-speaking areas) • German Society for Positive Psychology Research • French and Francophone Positive Psychology Association (Francophone areas) • Czech Positive Psychology Center • Hellenic Association of Positive Psychology • Italian Society of Positive Psychology • Polish Positive Psychology Association • Portuguese Association for Studies and Intervention in Positive Psychology • Spanish Society for Positive Psychology (SEPP) • Swiss Positive Psychology Association • Turkish Positive Psychology Association	• Oslo Summer School (Norway) • Aarhus University (Denmark) • Universiteit Twente; Maastricht University (The Netherlands) • Universidade de Lisboa (Portugal) • IE University (Spain) • University of East London; City University of London; University of Glasgow; Middlesex • University London; Anglia Ruskin University; Buckinghamshire New University (UK)

(*Continued*)

Table 7.1 (Continued)

	Associations	Courses and Degrees
Asia	• Asian Center for Applied Positive Psychology • Global Chinese Positive Psychology Association • National Positive Psychology Association, India • Japan Positive Psychology Association • Informal groups in South Korea	• Lebanese American University (Lebanon) • The Chinese University of Hong Kong; Hong Kong Shue Yan University (Hong Kong) • Jerusalem University (Israel) • School of Positive Psychology (Singapore)
Americas	• Associação de Psicologia Positiva da América Latina (Latin America) • Western Positive Psychology Association • Canadian Positive Psychology Association • Informal groups in Mexico and Brazil	• Instituto Chileno de Psicologia Positiva (Chile) • Universidad Iberoamericana (Mexico) • TechMillenio University (Mexico) • Claremont Graduate University; • University of Pennsylvania; University of Utah; • Harvard University; • Stanford University; University of California Los Angeles [UCLA] Extension; • University of Michigan, Case Western Reserve University, • University of Missouri (US)
Oceania	• New Zealand Association of Positive Psychology	• University of Sydney; • University of Melbourne; • RMIT University; • TAFE South Australia
Africa		• North-West University (South Africa)
International/ Global		• International Positive Psychology Association

Kim et al. (2018) / Reproduced with permission of International Journal of Wellbeing.

Mihaly clearly inspired millions of people around the world to focus their precious attention on positive psychology topics such as flow, optimal experience, well-being, peak performance, and human flourishing. He has helped us understand the importance of using scientific methods to advance knowledge and to develop effective evidence-based positive psychology interventions. He modeled as our founder and one of our top thought leaders how to use positive psychology to be a positively energizing leader (Cameron 2021), and he has shown us the importance of using scientific findings from peer-reviewed positive psychology research to improve our everyday lives, well-being, work, education, and societies across the globe (Donaldson et al. 2020). He has helped me and others develop frameworks that reflect and summarize this new scientific knowledge such as PERMA+4 (Donaldson and Donaldson 2024; Donaldson et al. 2022, 2023, 2024; Martin and Donaldson 2024), and has shown us how to design applications and interventions that on average improve our lives, and under specific conditions transform our lives (Donaldson et al. 2021, 2023).

Criticisms of Positive Psychology

Mihaly was always ready to gently engage with those who asserted that positive psychology was fluff, or just more silly positive thinking or smiley face happy-ology. His founding partner Martin Seligman also welcomed discussion and debate about the credibility of the new field they created together. They both acknowledged criticism in science is a main driver of progress, and Professor Seligman admits he has "always welcomed critics and shunned ass-kissers" (Seligman 2018, p. 266). They and other leaders in the field have provided sound counter-arguments to some of the main critiques and have also expressed their frustration when criticisms of positive psychology have been weak or even baseless by critics who have not done their homework – especially when critics have provided a list of debatable or inaccurate criticisms of positive psychology based on faulty logic and sloppy data (see Donaldson 2020; Gaffaney and Donaldson 2024; Seligman 2018, pp. 257–278).

In an effort to understand the critics and criticisms of positive psychology in more depth, I (Stewart) joined an international team of researchers focused on conducting and publishing the first systematic review on this topic (Van Zyl et al. 2023). The review identified 117 unique criticisms and critiques that we grouped into 21 categories, which culminated into the six themes shown in Figure 7.2.

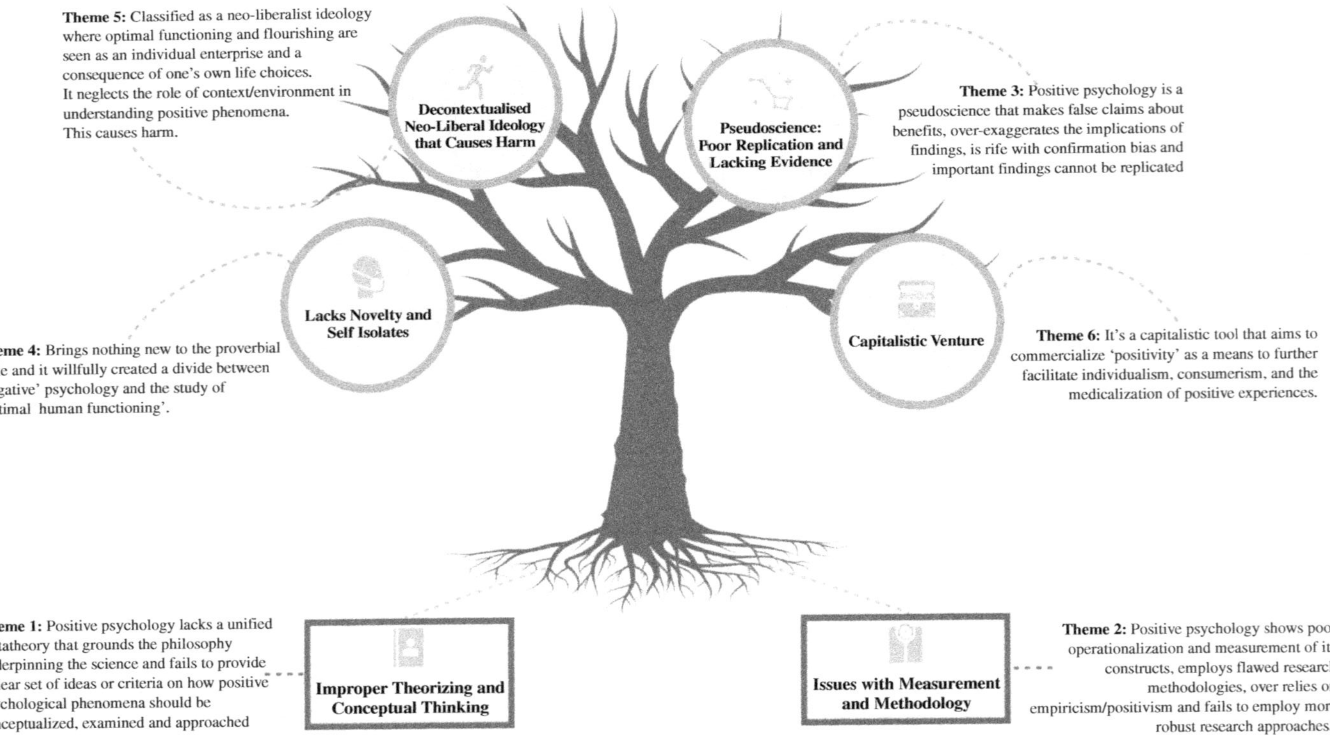

Figure 7.2 Summary of main criticisms and critiques of positive psychology.

In a subsequent project I worked with one of my colleagues on the original team to provide researchers with recommendations for how to evaluate the validity of the criticisms and critiques (Gaffaney and Donaldson 2024). We did this is the spirit of what Mihaly taught us – carefully looking at the evidence and both sides of each argument. Our recommendations were in the form of two checklists, one for researchers and another for practitioners. Our aim was to be both mindful of the past critical narrative around positive psychology and to help shape a more optimistic future narrative by providing possible solutions for improving future studies and practical applications of the science of positive psychology. It was real loss not having Mihaly to talk to about this project, but I feel confident he would have appreciated this balanced process and agreed with the conclusion that the science of positive psychology has continued to improve over time and is likely to have a very bright future in terms of improving the human condition.

He Wanted Us to Share with the World the Power Flow Theory and Flow 2.0

When Mihaly began his research into what became universally known as *flow,* the field of positive psychology did not yet exist. His long-time beloved colleague at Claremont Graduate University and another mentor of mine (Matt), Dr. Jeanne Nakamura, gave a perfect summation of the variety of his work: "The topics are varied but the work all expresses a single perspective on human functioning that was shaped by an unusual life and influences beyond psychological science—history, philosophy, and the arts." He spent his early years in Europe – born in what is now Croatia, then moving to Italy when his father opened a restaurant, traveling through Switzerland – before moving to the US at the age of 22 to pursue a career in psychology. This background was the ideal supplement to his autotelic mind.

One pursuit would open the door to new interests, people, and places, such as attending a talk on UFO sightings in Switzerland, where he heard Carl Jung speak about the traumatized psyches of Europeans after World War II that resulted in them projecting UFO sightings in the sky, which then spearheaded his interest in psychology. He was profoundly curious about what the world had to offer in the physical, intellectual, and spiritual realm, which would inform his approach to research for the duration of his life, enabling him to see unique patterns in human experience.

In the initial flow studies, his interviews included individuals that, on its surface, were experts in domains that had very little in common – painting, dancing, surgery, rock climbing, science, and chess – and developed the dimensions of the flow state based on their unifying elements. Mihaly was an avid rock climber himself in his younger years, which served as one of his primary sources of flow; in his later years, his flow experiences became more of an intellectual pursuit.

Having developed my close relationship with him in his later years, I (Matt) was constantly blown away by Mihaly's own openness to intellectual experience. He listened intently to every student's ideas, considered their words carefully, and would also give a reply that expanded the conversation. Having Mihaly listen to one of my ideas about flow with thought and care was my personal version of what I imagine a young musician would feel like if Taylor Swift listened to one of their songs and gave feedback.

Along with his openness, another quality that continuously struck me was his lack of ego. He once told me, when I asked him about what it was like having presidents and Super Bowl winning coaches applying his ideas, "Flow belongs to all of us." It was as if he saw himself as more of an archaeologist of ideas, digging through human experience and discovering this unifying state of optimal functioning, which he then presented to the world. He never acted like he "owned" flow or that his name should always be associated with the ideas. He was a man of striking humility. That humility was the natural outcome of pursuing experiences and ideas for their own sake, because of his natural interests or the sense of enjoyment and meaning they provided. He actually *showed* us what an autotelic life of intrinsic pursuit looks like, and the impact that made on the lives he touched. When I started studying with him, I mainly admired him for ideas and his work, but by the end, I admired him most for his character, kindness, and generosity of spirit.

In our conversations about the future of flow, he expressed genuine interest in the various digital frontiers that had the power to enable and inhibit flow, but also expressed a wish that we didn't lose sight of the more mundane moments of human experience that could contain meaning. In his book *Creativity* (1996), he shares this advice:

> *Try to be surprised by something every day. It could be something you see, hear, or read about. Stop to look at the unusual car parked at the curb, taste the new item on the cafeteria menu, actually listen to your colleague at the office. How is this different from other similar cars, dishes or conversations? What is its essence? Don't assume that you*

already know what these things are all about, or that even if you knew them, they wouldn't matter anyway. Experience this one thing for what it is, not what you think it is. Be open to what the world is telling you. Life is nothing more than a stream of experiences – the more widely and deeply you swim in it, the richer your life will be.

His approach to what makes a good life – controlling the contents of consciousness and fully investing ourselves in experiences that challenge us – reframes many of the stereotypes of what it means to be happy. If I were to ask you, "Picture a person who is happy," we would most likely think of a person smiling or laughing. In the stereotype of a happy person, they are thinking mainly positive thoughts, often relaxing without a care in the world. However, the experiences that make up a truly worthwhile life usually often look nothing like this. Happiness can look like a person deep in thought, a grunt while serving a tennis ball, a verbal exchange of ideas, or closing our eyes while performing a violin solo.

Mihaly's work added a new chapter to the book of happiness that has been at the forefront of human thought and desire for thousands of years. In Chapter 1 of *Flow,* titled "Happiness Revisited," he opens with, "Twenty-three hundred years ago Aristotle concluded that, more than anything else, men and women seek happiness. While happiness itself is sought after for its own sake, every other goal – health, beauty, money, or power – is valued only because we expect that it will make us happy" (p. 1).

The sway of these external rewards as conduits toward happiness only continues to grow more powerful with the current ubiquity of social media, where every day it always seems like someone is taking better vacations (Instagram), making more money or climbing the corporate ladder more quickly (LinkedIn), or living it up with a gaggle of close friends (TikTok). We know more than ever about what truly makes us happy, but our culture is largely set up to encourage us to ignore the research. If we control the contents of consciousness on our own, we won't need to buy as many products or track the lives of others. This is why I put the following quote above my desk in my home office – it is my favorite line from his work and serves as a constant reminder to myself:

The best moments in our lives are not the passive, receptive, relaxing times... The best moments usually occur if a person's body or mind is stretched to its limits in a voluntary effort to accomplish something difficult and worthwhile.

(Csikszentmihalyi 1990, p. 3)

In conversations with Mihaly, he would say there is no "Flow switch" we can turn on and off – it takes a substantial amount of self-discipline and the right surrounding circumstances to increase its likelihood. Like all worthwhile things in life – being a good parent, having a happy marriage, sustaining a fulfilling career – it takes a lot of small things done well consistently over time, and your version of how you accomplish them will be unique to you. While we can have isolated flow experiences doing certain activities, Mihaly's wish was that people would pursue a more holistic approach to flow – where we wouldn't need to "find it" per se, but it would *find us* because of how we approached daily experience, by approaching all that life has to offer with an open mind, seeking experiences for their own sake, devoting ourselves fully to what's in front of us, and not succumbing to the power of ego. As Albert Einstein said, "Ego=1/Knowledge. More the knowledge lesser the ego, lesser the knowledge more the ego."

With that approach, life's more ordinary moments – a conversation with a barista, walking our dog, a trip to the grocery store – can take on a vitality that considerably contribute to a joyful life. This was Mihaly's approach to life, and in his understated way, his character and ideas inspired millions of people to alter their approach. While the experiences that humans pursue to make up a flow-driven life will inevitably shift as technology continues to advance, Mihaly's ideas are evergreen. When it comes down to it, a flow-driven life is more about character and values than a pursuit of a particular activity – curiosity, openness to experience, generosity, discipline, willpower, and gratitude (to name a few). When interacting with others, for example, flow ensues when we treat them with kindness and respect, deeply listening to their thoughts and stories, asking questions that expand the conversation and ultimately deepen the connection. Successfully adapting to the digital future will require learning new skills to match a fresh set of challenges, skills that many of us will be reluctant to learn. Achieving mastery over these new sets of skills will undoubtedly contain moments of frustration, as new modes of technology will fundamentally alter the contents of our consciousness and how we direct our attention. However, if we use Mihaly's ideas as inspiration and his life as an example, there is an opportunity to broaden the possibilities of optimal experience and develop into more complex beings.

Conclusion

Mihaly has clearly left us the legacy he envisioned. He would love all of us to continue using his ideas to make our lives better so we have the capacity to be a positive influence on others' lives. The cumulative and evolving peer-reviewed positive psychological science deepening our understanding of human flourishing, optimal experience, well-being, and what makes life worth living traces back to his bold vision of a more balanced approach to behavioral science research. He trained hundreds of graduate students and junior colleagues and helped to build a worldwide community of positive psychologists to continue to push his more balanced agenda (e.g., studying strengths and opportunities, as well as deficits and problems) in the face of the many headwinds and sometimes hostile critics of positive psychology (Gaffaney and Donaldson 2024).

It is important to mention as we close this chapter that he also had an even more bold aspiration for positive psychological science and the future of humankind. He shared this aspiration in his profound chapter "Positive Psychology and a Positive Worldview: A New Hope for the Future of Humankind" (Csikszentmihalyi 2020). Despite the massive challenges facing societies across the globe, our great leader and colleague remained hopeful that the science of positive psychology would eventually evolve at scale and provide us with a collective new human self-image. He persuasively provided us with a very thoughtful historical and anthropological analysis of the evolution of our self-image and concluded that the intangible and almost invisible difference positive psychological science is likely to make is proving a new understanding of what it means to be human.

> *We are about to change – I shall argue – our vision of the human condition from one of the dismal pessimism to a vision that foregrounds what is good about women and men and provides ideas and processes that will nurture, cultivate, and increase what is good about us and our actions. And this change is likely to pay dividends in many areas of life from the economy to the arts and from politics to religion.*
>
> *(Csikszentmihalyi 2020, p. 256)*

Say more, you might ask. How can positive psychological science help provide a more positive and productive image of humankind to advance our humanity? Mihaly thought it was time to evolve beyond some of the popular images of humankind left behind by earlier world-views provided by imminent psychologists. For example, he thought it was time to integrate but evolve beyond the views of laboratory experimentation (Wilhelm Wundt 1832–1920), behaviorism and learning theory (John B. Watson 1878–1958), psychoanalysis (Sigmund Freud 1856–1939), cognitivism (Jean Piaget 1950–2000), and the like by:

- "using the knowledge and techniques that psychology has developed so far but at the same time taking into account that human consciousness is a new phenomenon, with its sui generis organization and possibilities, therefore nonreductionistic explanations are necessary to understand human behavior
- "realizing the future will depend on the decisions we are making in the present, therefore psychology cannot be neutral about the consequences of human action
- "taking serious the best of the past, for example, the experience of earlier generations codified in older sources of wisdom" (Csikszentmihalyi 2020, p. 263)

While he often told us he believed positive psychology was more successful in the first 25 years than he could have even imagined when he founded it, he was not content and wanted to give as much energy as he could muster toward continuing to shape its future. Mihaly did just that until he could no longer meaningfully contribute. But even then, he was so enthusiastic about what positive psychology would become in the future – how it would all turn out. Well my friends, it is all up to us now that he has passed. He has given us a wonderful gift that we can continue to use to help ourselves function as our best selves more often, and to make the largest positive impact we can on others and society. So let's get to work and begin to answer his next set of major research questions:

We are responsible for our lives, so:
How can we learn to live happier and more meaningful lives?

We are shapers of our future, so:
In which directions should we help steer evolution?

We are the stewards of our world, so:
How can we achieve sustainable harmony on the planet? (Csikszentmihalyi 2020, p. 264)

References

Cameron, K. (2021) Positively energizing leadership. Oakland, CA: Berrett-Koehler.

Csikszentmihalyi, M. (1990). *Flow: The Psychology of Optimal Experience.* New York: HarperCollins.

Csikszentmihalyi, M. (1996). *Creativity: Flow and the Psychology of Discovery and Invention.* New York: HarperCollins.

Csikszentmihalyi, M. (2020). Positive psychology and a positive worldview: New hope for the future of humankind. In S. I. Donaldson, M. Csikszentmihalyi, and J. Nakamura (eds.), *Positive Psychological Science: Improving Everyday Life, Well-Being, Work, Education, and Society* (2nd ed.). New York: Routledge Academic.

Donaldson, S. I. (2020). Using positive psychological science to design and evaluate interventions. In S. I. Donaldson, M. Csikszentmihalyi, and J. Nakamura (eds.), *Positive Psychological Science: Improving Everyday Life, Well-Being, Work, Education, and Society* (2nd ed.). New York: Routledge Academic.

Donaldson, S. I. and Donaldson, S. I. (2018). Other people matter: The power of positive relationships. In Warren, M. A. and S. I. Donaldson. *Toward a Positive Psychology of Relationships: Theory and Research.* Westport, CT: Praeger.

Donaldson, S. I. and Donaldson, S. I. (2024, in press). PERMA+4 and positive organizational psychology 2.0: Opportunities for embracing methodological and technological innovations.

Donaldson, S. I., Cabrera, V., and Gaffaney, J. (2021). Following the science to generate well-being: Using the highest quality experimental evidence to design interventions. *Frontiers in Psychology.* https://doi.org/10.3389/fpsyg.2021.739352

Donaldson, S. I., Csikszentmihalyi, M., and Nakamura, J. (2020). *Positive Psychological Science: Improving Everyday Life, Well-Being, Work, Education, and Society* (2nd ed.). New York: Routledge Academic.

Donaldson, S. I., Dollwet, M., and Rao, M. (2015). Happiness, excellence, and optimal human functioning revisited: Examining the peer-reviewed literature linked to positive psychology. *Journal of Positive Psychology* 9(6): 1–11.

Donaldson, S. I., Gaffaney, J., and Caberra, V. (2023). The science and practice of positive psychology: From a bold vision to PERMA+4. In C. Markey and H. S. Friedman (eds.), *The 3rd Edition of the Encyclopedia of Mental Health.* Cambridge, MA: Academic Press.

Donaldson, S. I., Van Zyl, L. E., and Donaldson, S. I. (2022). PERMA+4: A framework for work-related well-being, performance and positive organizational psychology 2.0. *Frontiers in Psychology* 12: 817244. https://doi.org/10.3389/fpsyg.2021.817244

Donaldson, S.I., Donaldson, S.I., McQuaid, M.L., and Kern, M.L. (2024). Systems-informed PERMA+4: Measuring well-being and performance at the employee, team, and supervisor levels of analysis. *International Journal of Applied Positive Psychology*.

Einstein, A. *Albert Einstein quotes. Good Reads*. https://www.goodreads.com/quotes/1008163-ego-1-knowledge-more-the-knowledge-lesser-the-ego-lesser-the

Gaffaney, J. and Donaldson, S. I. (2024). Evaluating criticisms and critiques: Recommendations for improving the science & practice of positive psychology. Manuscript under review.

Hertzog, C. (2023, April 24). Review: Midori masterfully plays Bach's solo violin music for La Jolla music society. *The San Diego Union-Tribune*. Retrieved from https://www.sandiegouniontribune.com/2023/04/24/midori-masterfully-plays-bachs-solo-violin-music-for-la-jolla-music-society/

Kim, H., Doiron, K., Warren, M., and Donaldson, S. (2018). The international landscape of positive psychology research: a systematic review. *International Journal of Wellbeing* 8(1): 50–70. https://doi.org/10.5502/ijw.v8i1.651

Martin, D. and Donaldson, S. I. (2024). Lessons from debates about foundational positive psychology theories & frameworks: Positivity Ratio, Broaden & Build, Happiness Pie, PERMA to PERMA+4. *Journal of Positive Psychology*: 1–15, https://doi.org/10.1080/17439760.2024.2325452

Seligman, M.E.P. (2018). PERMA and the building blocks of well-being. *Journal of Positive Psychology* 13(4): 333–335. https://doi.org/10.1080/17439760.2018.1437466

Steimer, S. (2021, October 28). Mihaly Csikszentmihalyi, pioneering psychologist and "father of flow," 1934–2021. Uchicago News. https://news.uchicago.edu/story/mihaly-csikszentmihalyi-pioneering-psychologist-and-father-flow-1934-2021

Van Zyl, L., Gaffaney, J., Van der Vaart, L., Dik, B., and Donaldson, S. I. (2023). The critiques and criticisms of positive psychology: A systematic review. *Journal of Positive Psychology*.

We highly encourage you to read the original works of Mihaly Csikszentmihalyi. Please find a list of his articles, chapters, and books on Google Scholar: https://scholar.google.com/citations?hl=en&user=ycPRZqAAAAAJ. We have provided a selected list of his books below to help you get started.

Selected Books by Mihaly Csikszentmihalyi

Beyond Boredom & Anxiety 1975
Flow: The Psychology of Optimal Experience 1991
Flow: The Psychology of Happiness 1992
The Evolving Self 1993
Creativity: Flow and the Psychology of Discovery and Invention 1996
Finding Flow: The Psychology of Engagement with Everyday Life 1997
Flow: The Classic Work on How to Achieve Happiness 2002
Good Work: When Excellence and Ethics Meet 2002
Good Business: Leadership, Flow, and the Making of Meaning 2004
Experience Sampling Method: Measuring the Quality of Everyday Life 2006
The Systems Model of Creativity: The Collected Works of Mihaly Csikszentmihalyi 2014
Flow and Foundations of Positive Psychology 2014
Applications of Flow in Human Development: The Collected Works of Mihaly Csikszentmihalyi 2014
Positive Psychological Science: Improving Everyday Life, Well-being, Work, Education and Societies Across the Globe 2020
Flow 2.0: Optimal Experience in a Complex World. Honoring Mihaly Csikszentmihalyi's Legacy 2024

Index

Note: Page numbers with figures in *italic* and tables in **bold**.

Flow 2.0: Optimal Experience in a Complex World. Honoring Mihaly Csikszentmihalyi's Legacy, First Edition. Stewart I. Donaldson and Matthew Dubin.
© 2025 John Wiley & Sons Ltd. Published 2025 by John Wiley & Sons Ltd.

p

r

www.ingramcontent.com/pod-product-compliance
Lightning Source LLC
Chambersburg PA
CBHW052053120425
25012CB00012B/56
9781394262991